PENGUIN BOOKS
ALL THAT YOU CAN'T LEAVE BEHIND

Soumya Bhattacharya's first book, *You Must Like Cricket?*, was published to acclaim across the world in 2006. He is also the author of the novel *If I Could Tell You*. His writing has appeared in the *New York Times* in the US; the *Sydney Morning Herald* and the *Age* (Melbourne) in Australia; and the *Guardian*, the *Observer*, the *Independent*, the *New Statesman* and *Wisden* in the UK. He is the Editor of the *Hindustan Times*'s Mumbai edition. He lives with his wife and daughter in Mumbai.

PRAISE FOR *YOU MUST LIKE CRICKET?*

'Beautifully written . . . Bhattacharya uses his anecdotes tellingly to flesh out his argument about the way cricket has taken hold of a country'
Times (London)

'Heir to a tradition harking back to cricket's first literary classic . . . Highly entertaining'
Mike Marqusee, *Guardian* (London)

'A wonderful homage to Indian cricket . . . exceptional'
Birmingham Post

'Lovingly written . . . fascinating. Some mouldering clichés are chucked out'
The Wisden Cricketer

'An engaging book, with plenty of verve and charm. The subtitle—*Memoirs of an Indian Cricket Fan*—could easily (and accurately) be rejigged to Memoirs of Every Indian'
TimeOut

'It's not so much about cricket as about an obsession. It is an illumination of the place cricket holds in the minds of most of us. Even if your answer to the question in the title is a resounding NO, you like the book'
Hindustan Times

'An amusing and thoughtful memoir . . . an engaging chronicle by someone who knows not only cricket but his country and the wider world'
Age (Melbourne)

'Bhattacharya writes in a fluid, conversational style . . . [Renders] the intimate intensity of the fan's world while also placing it in a broader context'
Sydney Morning Herald

all that you can't leave behind

WHY WE CAN NEVER
DO WITHOUT CRICKET

SOUMYA
BHATTACHARYA

PENGUIN BOOKS

An imprint of Penguin Random House

PENGUIN BOOKS

USA | Canada | UK | Ireland | Australia
New Zealand | India | South Africa | China | Singapore

Penguin Books is part of the Penguin Random House group of companies
whose addresses can be found at global.penguinrandomhouse.com

Published by Penguin Random House India Pvt. Ltd
4th Floor, Capital Tower 1, MG Road,
Gurugram 122 002, Haryana, India

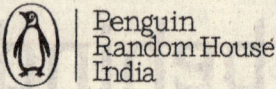

Penguin
Random House
India

First published by Penguin Books India 2009

ISBN 9780143066293

Typeset in Bembo by Mantra Virtual Services, New Delhi

Printed at Repro India Limited

www.penguin.co.in

MIX
Paper from
responsible sources
FSC® C047271

To Oishi,

For her eighth

But where then is the mirror? Where shall we go to find our face?

—Milan Kundera, *The Curtain*

Shey taa ki bhaalo naa khaaraap? (So is that a good thing or a bad thing?)

—A character in Satyajit Ray's film
Seemabaddha (Company Limited)

Contents

Contents

Just
Where
Were
You
When
It
Happened?

In the decades to come, that instant on the evening of Monday, 24 September 2007, will become a conversational touchstone, a sort of Kennedy moment for most Indians. Where were you when Sreesanth, running back from short fine leg, caught Misbah-ul-Haq off Joginder Sharma in the final over of the World Twenty20 Championship final at the Wanderer's in Johannesburg?

As I write it reminds me—in kind but not of course in degree—of that *other* moment, *the* Kennedy One in Indian cricket (in Indian sport, in modern Indian popular culture. Are they all the same thing?): *where* were you on Saturday, 25 June 1983, when India won the World Cup final against West Indies at Lord's?

There have arguably been greater, more famous victories (and with cricket fans, arguing about these things is going down a dangerous road. We can spend months on a desert island replaying and pitting India v West Indies, Port of Spain 1976, against

India v Australia, Eden Gardens 2001) than the Prudential Cup win in 1983, but if I were to somehow pin down the instant when India's love affair with cricket took a turn for the passionate, overriding, nation- and nationalism-defying obsession that it has become, I'd go back to that summer's evening in Lord's, that night in India turned as vivid and brilliant as day by the fireworks that wouldn't stop and the streams of people on the streets.

I remember the grins. There *he* was, with a smile that couldn't quite make up its mind about whether to take seriously what was happening, his hands wrapped around a trophy that no Indian had ever believed he would get his hands on. (And hasn't since.)

Kapil Dev: India's captain with the Prudential World Cup. And there they all were, grinning like they had never grinned before: Kapil's Devils, world champions.

Where *were* you?

For millions of fans like me, the details of that day (and the celebrations as the night deepened) are imprinted on our minds in the way our most precious memories are. Philip Roth had once said that our memories of the past are not memories of facts but memories of our imaginings of the facts. In this instance, he was wrong. These memories, for us, *are* the facts, every single one of them. And they are so grounded in truth that we, more than a quarter of a century on, are still resolutely holding on to every one of them.

It was *that* kind of day, you see. It was *that* kind of night.

I was thirteen years old and had watched the game in our south Kolkata home. We watched it, my parents and I, on the bed, the pillows puffed up against the bedstead. The TV, a newly acquired black-and-white set, had a varnished wooden body and an intimidating, long, delicate aerial that got in the way when we negotiated the narrow strip of floor between the bed and the TV. It sat on a table with a wobbly leg.

My mother had allowed the curtains of the bedroom to be lowered so that a couple of dozen boys from the slum down the road could clamber on to each other's shoulders and watch the cricket. This was, remember, 1983, and not every slum had a TV set of its own. In fact, many middle-class homes, like ours, had just got one.

I listened on radio to the moments on which the match turned—Viv Richards pulling Madan Lal, mistiming it a fraction and Kapil Dev running backwards, running with the sun in his eyes and his heart in his hands till he had caught the ball—at a restaurant in south Kolkata. I was there for a takeaway.

I had given up the match for lost, and offered to go and fetch dinner, abandoning the TV at home, and my parents who were enduring the game with heroic stoicism.

There was no other customer, only surly waiters who seemed suddenly transformed, incredulous and delighted at the fall of the wicket. I whooped and cheered, and began to run around the deserted restaurant, arms outstretched, doing the aeroplane imitation I had perfected as a little boy. The waiters too joined me.

Let me remind you exactly how that match had gone. Not that, if you are one of those fans like me who think of cities in terms of their cricket grounds, you'll need any reminding. But who am I to assume that you are? How can I tell why you are reading this? Perhaps you are because this is not so much a book about cricket as *around* cricket, because this is a book about India more than anything else.

Whatever, as some people say. The point is that these things—so unforgettable, and perhaps more sharply delicious in remembrance than in their actual occurrence—these things bear repetition.

Fans like me never tire of it.

Batting first on losing the toss, India was all out for 183 in that sixty-overs-a-side match. Our innings was most memorable for one stroke that Krishnamachari Srikanth played (imagine, Indian limited-overs cricket was still as much of a toddler for us to remember a team's innings for one batsman's shot; think of how meagre our expectations were like back then, and of how easily we were delighted). Well, there was Srikanth, at the beginning of the Indian innings, down on one knee, taking Andy Roberts from well outside off stump and sending the ball screaming to the fence.

In real terms, that cavalier boundary—and the five subsequent ones that Srikanth thumped—did not help things along too much. India was all out for the sort of total that the West Indies, the defending world champions, were expected to overhaul without even bothering to break into a trot.

When I had left for the restaurant, West Indies seemed to be precisely on course, with the sort of commanding disdain that they had patented in their reign as the best team in the world. First, though, came a big surprise. It took aback everyone, not least, I suspect, Balwinder Singh Sandhu, who delivered India's ball of the tournament.

It was the twelfth ball that Gordon Greenidge faced in his innings. It pitched outside the off stump. It curled in. (With Sandhu, it always curled in, never ripped or jagged back.) Greenidge underestimated the curl. He shouldered his arms. And he was bowled.

It must have been the uncharitable who later floated the story (apocryphal, surely?) that the ball did so much because it had hit a pebble on the pitch.

We weren't allowed to think of it as a portent. Viv Richards had come in appeared to be in the mood for carnage.

Cutting, pulling, driving, languorous yet lethal, he was reducing the Indian bowling to shreds. Oh, the Blakean fearful symmetry of his shots on either side, the imperiousness. It made you want to genuflect—not to beg for mercy, but to display devotion—even as he was murdering your team.

His wicket—the one that I listened to on radio at the restaurant—was the pivot on which the game turned. By the time I returned home with naan and mutton do piaza, West Indies was 66 for 5.

The unbelievable was happening in front of our eyes—on the new black-and-white TV.

And all we could do was sit on the bed, transfixed, spooning curry into our mouths with the naan, not looking at where the food was being shovelled, not quite, and not really minding when bits of the food dribbled on to the crisp, white sheet.

And then it came, *that* moment: Michael Holding swivelled and turned away and Mohinder Amarnath was running down the pitch and there were Kapil and Yashpal Sharma and Sandip Patil all in a mad scramble for the stumps as thousands and thousands poured into the ground and the players weaved in and out, seemingly afloat on a sea of people, on their way to the pavilion.

I remember this too. Do you? The spray of champagne from the balcony; the droplets catching and refracting the sunlight. Or is that merely an imagined version of my memory of the fact?

How exactly did it happen? (I have wondered about this so many times—and especially after a much-vaunted India has been walloped, *again*, in a World Cup game in the recent past.) How?

India was certainly not the most talented side of the 1983 championship. (We've had several better teams since.) It had no track record of one-day cricket success. It had had far less practice in the abbreviated form of the game than, say, England or Australia.

We had great players like Kapil and brave ones like Mohinder Amarnath. India was lucky. India was plucky. (Remember, we beat the world champions not once, but twice—on the first occasion, earlier on in the tournament.) But more than anything else, everything came together that glorious English summer in a way things on occasion do in team sport: when all the units in the side click into place, when someone always, somehow rises to the occasion, one player inspires the others, that rare chemistry is set off, when the cliché of one for all and all for one becomes a demonstrable, successful, world-beating, world-changing reality.

Well, at least it changed the world for us. For ever.

It gave Indian cricket the confidence to believe that it could compete, that nothing was impossible.

It's always tempting—and just as often misleading—to look for a moment when something became a trend, a habit, an obsession, when something *really* began. It's silly because nothing actually happens in isolation; every instant has a context, is anchored to the past, to what has come before it. T.S. Eliot put it best in his 1922 essay, 'Tradition and the Individual Talent', when he said that we must be aware not merely of the pastness of the past, but also its presence. Yet, the temptation to look for A Moment is hard to not yield to.

India has been playing international cricket since 1932. But if I were to look for an instant when cricket became India's very own game, when the notion of cricket defining India and India defining world cricket was born, I'd have to go back to 25 June 1983.

It has been nearly twenty-six years now. And look at where we have come.

On the evening of the final in Johannesburg in September 2007, we had all given up the match for lost, and then counted it won, and then given it up for lost again and then, never mind, stopped thinking about what would happen because what was happening, each moment, the frenzied exciting succession of moments, was swallowing everything else up, leaving no room for contemplation—or hope or fear or doubt.

I was in the Mumbai office of the *Hindustan Times*, the newspaper I work for. There we were, a hundred-odd people on our floor: the know-alls and the know-nothings; the ones who take pleasure in saying they don't care about the game; the ones who think it's left field to say that it's not only they who don't bother but *no one at all* bothers about cricket that much any longer (why, didn't we notice, football was becoming the new cricket?); and the ones who reference point their lives with cricket and are the real sceptics of the Twenty20 format.

No, this wasn't cricket as we adored it, this wasn't, well, cricket at all, we the Twenty20 sceptics said, but when the moment came and the men in blue took the field and play started, we simply couldn't bear to turn away. It's work, we told each other quietly, we've got a newspaper to put out, and there is no news more worth paying attention to tonight than this game.

It was the same in every office around India. Or at least in the ones in which people had had to stay back between 5.30 p.m. and 8.45 p.m. The rush hour that day was at half-past three: the rush to get home from work, fix the drinks, open the packets of munchies, get to the sofa in front of the TV.

Our office was like a mini-stadium: the same collective desire that makes the atmosphere crackle with electricity; the shared keenness of everybody wanting the same thing and no one daring to hope too much for it.

And then—as Diwali arrived in Delhi and Durga Puja in Kolkata before they were due, amid a flurry of fireworks and reason-defying abandon—not too long after the game had begun, Joginder Sharma (inexperienced, under pressure like never before, hero or villain for life over the course of the next few balls) took the final wicket and it was all over.

Or was it? Or had it all merely begun?

Over the following days, culminating in the team's homecoming and triumphant victory procession from Mumbai's airport to the city's southernmost tip, talk of a New India, a Young India, a Fearless India playing without fear of vertigo after having climbed higher than anybody could have expected became the delirious staple of Indian public life and discourse.

The urchin who had watched the game with his

nose pressed against the window of a shop front on Gariahat Road in Kolkata, the industrialist popping Dom Perignon at the Taj Mahal hotel in Mumbai, the sniffy executive who pretended she couldn't see why there should be such a fuss about cricket, were all borne aloft and swept away in the wave of generosity and self-congratulation.

And we, the sceptics? We smiled indulgently, we said this wasn't quite a *real* triumph as triumphs go (oh, no, this wasn't even *comparable* to the Tests won in Adelaide in 2003 and Multan the year after), and waited for the cheerleaders of Dhoni's side to start saying—after the first falter of the same team—how this was a bunch of overpaid, talentless, arrogant young men who model for consumer durables when they ought to be out on the field, sweating it out in practice.

The sceptics did acknowledge something that night. We were well aware of the fact that the men who comprised the heart of this team would in time hold in their hands Indian cricket's future. They were the men who would first comprise the national one-day side with an eye on the World Cup in 2011. And in time would take over from the presiding legends—Sachin Tendulkar, Rahul Dravid, V.V.S. Laxman, Sourav Ganguly and Anil Kumble, the stalwarts of our most sensational, most vaunted triumphs in international cricket—in Tests, the most challenging version of the game.

The future was here; and we could do nothing but embrace it.

I am no fan of Twenty20 cricket, but I can see why people love it, why it's such a smash hit. It's short and exciting; it simplifies the game, makes it more inclusive and opens it up to a new, wider audience. No one has the time for the five-day version any longer, the world has moved on, our lives are on fast forward, and we can't afford to track a game over the better part of a week. (This last argument is as puerile as it is philistine. It's like saying because it takes so long, we shouldn't pay any heed to literature, we should consign James and Flaubert and Dostoevsky and Updike and Roth to the dustbin, and stick to only reading text messages on our mobile phones, status updates on Facebook and Twitter, and menus at restaurants.)

Twenty20 doesn't work for me because it whittles down the unique soul of cricket: its sense of narrative, of the contemplation that it offers, of the stringing out of things on a long high wire of protracted drama and tension, of its sense of slowly unfolding drama over days.

But I am aware that I sound anachronistic. Twenty20 is the future of the game—or at least it will be the cornerstone of the popularity of cricket in the future. Conceptualized by the Indian cricket board (no surprises there) and backed by the International Cricket Council, the Indian Premier League—a Twenty20 tournament of eight teams comprising players from all over the world who were bought, American football-style, at auctions by franchisees of the teams—has ended a successful second season in South Africa, after a hugely popular, world-attention-grabbing first season in 2008. It is becoming a tournament that is beginning to redefine the boundaries and the very notion of the game.

Who knows, this may well be the form of cricket that my daughter, now eight, will grow up to admire. Of course, it helps—and it will help—that India won the World Twenty20 Championship in 2007. (I remember how we overnight became devotees of the one-day game after winning the World Cup in 1983. It turned out that we had previously scoffed at it not so much because we were purists but because we were hopeless at it.)

The biggest thing Twenty20 has going for it is that it is a version of cricket, and in India any version will do. In our collective consciousness and in our popular culture, there is nothing quite like cricket. There never will be. And we are always happy, almost all of us, to make room for it, any version of it, and welcome it into our midst.

It's
Our
Game,
and
It
Belongs
to
Us

In the opening pages of *A Season with Verona* (a riveting account of following the Italian football team, Hellas Verona, through one league season), Tim Parks tells us of the etymology of the word 'fan'. It comes, he writes, 'from fanatic, from the Latin fanaticus, which means a worshipper at a temple'.

It's particularly appropriate, that origin, when it comes to talking about cricket and India, because one of the truisms we have about cricket is that it is like a religion for us. (You tend to see these silly placards at stadiums too; a misleading platitude masquerading as an original aphorism.)

Cricket like religion in India? Oh no, it isn't. 'Religion,' as Christopher Hitchens wrote in his 2007 book, *God is not Great: How Religion Poisons Everything*, is 'violent, irrational, intolerant, allied to racism, tribalism, and bigotry, invested in ignorance and hostile to free inquiry . . .'

Religion led to the bloodbath that accompanied the birth pangs of India or, more precisely, the birth pangs of the two nation states of India and Pakistan.

At least 200,000 people died. Religion led to riots that convulsed Mumbai and threatened to tear apart its secular fabric forever. It prompted the pogrom against Muslims in Gujarat—one of the worst pogroms in the history of modern India.

Religion has scarred India more deeply than anything else. Cricket is the balm that heals. Cricket is our anti-religion, our most precious, deeply secular institution.

That's a huge thing, but it's not the only reason why cricket is so essential, so central to our country.

As the most visible expression of national identity, as an obsession or a dream, cricket is the only thing that unites a country as diverse and as contradiction-fraught as India. Cricket is the glue that binds together the small minority of Indians who have access to the Internet and who are at the forefront of and the biggest beneficiaries of the country's economic growth, social change and IT revolution, and the huge percentage of the population that gets by on less than a dollar a day.

India, with its dizzying economic growth rate, is expected (notwithstanding the repercussions of a global economic downturn), along with China, to alter the geopolitical map of the world by well before the middle of this century. But the vertiginous growth is making wider the gulf between the educated urban elite (which is driving and thriving on India's rapid transformation) and the 70 per cent of the population that still lives in the country's vast rural hinterland.

The only thing that these two sections of India's population have in common is their passion for the game. Otherwise, they could well have been living in two different worlds. If the urchin on Mahim Causeway in Mumbai who watched the Twenty20 final in South Africa with his nose pressed to a shop front window were ever to meet the bloke who was popping celebratory champagne at the Taj Mahal Hotel that night, they would only ever have one thing to talk about: the cricket.

For a burgeoning, confident, aggressively consumerist metropolitan elite, cricket has fostered a strong sense of national identity. For these people, scornful of politicians and too self-absorbed to be really bothered with their shenanigans, the game has become the most triumphant mirror of the ideas of nation and patriotism.

For millions of Indians (the ones who live on minimum wages, never take holidays, have no other avenue of entertainment, can afford merely a community television on which to watch the matches), exulting in the success of eleven men on a green field is as close as they will themselves ever get to success. These Indians are not proud of their city, town or village, their backgrounds or their careers; they have little to look forward to in terms of what their country might have to offer them or what they might be able to give themselves. They have only the cricket.

So this game is to do with all of us. Remember India's tour of Australia in 2007–08? In January 2008, at the Sydney Cricket Ground in the second Test of the series, there was an exchange between the Australian all-rounder Andrew Symonds and the Indian off-spinner Harbhajan Singh. At the time, Harbhajan and Sachin Tendulkar were batting. The players on the field intervened; it seemed as though the matter had been sorted out. (That's what former Australia captain Steve Waugh afterwards said should have been done in the first place.) Or so we thought, till we found out that Australia captain Ricky Ponting had reported it to the umpires, and the Indian spinner was charged with having made racist remarks.

The umpires, we found afterwards, had heard nothing offensive. Tendulkar, batting at the other end, was certain that nothing offensive had been said. Harbhajan denied having said anything racist. There was no audio or video evidence. Ponting and his teammates were sure that the racist taunt had been made.

Probing the complaint, match referee Mike Procter was 'satisfied beyond a reasonable doubt that Harbhajan directed that word [monkey] at Symonds and also that he meant it to offend on the basis of Symonds's race or ethnic origin'. He ruled that Harbhajan was guilty and recommended a three-match ban. (But what did Procter base his judgement on? The Australians' words against the Indians'? We never found out, though it would have been good to know. That, though, is a different story and has little to do with what followed.)

The Indians appealed. At the hearing, the Indian defence was this: Harbhajan had used a Hindi swear word that *sounded* like 'monkey'. The defence was accepted. The charge was watered down to using offensive language that was not racist; Harbhajan's penalty turned out to be much lighter than what had been initially recommended.

As this drama unfolded on the field, waves of shrill, jingoistic, self-righteous anger swept through India. A scrap on a cricket field had turned into a clash of cultures and societies. The whole thing continued to feed on itself, grew bloated, assumed a character and an identity beyond the game of which they had been born, transmogrified into quite something else and—to borrow from Martin Amis on Salman Rushdie after the fatwa—disappeared into the world of block capitals of newspaper headlines and hysterical TV channel sound bites.

Nothing could be more appropriate than the fact that this clash—which had implications as much for the future of cricket as beyond the game—should be seen through the window of cricket, the sport that defines the world's most populous democracy.

The *Hindustan Times* conducted a nationwide poll about the whole affair. Only 14 per cent of the respondents thought that the continuing controversy was 'just about cricket'; 86 per cent believed it had wounded national pride.

Who said it was *just* a game anyway?

We take cricket seriously—and think of it in terms of things like national pride—because, among other things, cricket is really serious business now. The English writer Tim Adams, in a discussion of the professionalization and the commodification of tennis in his book *On Being John McEnroe*, turns to the cultural historian Johann Huizinga for an explanation of how things have become so: as players have become serious businessmen, mini-industries, 'a far-reaching contamination of play and serious activity has taken place. The two spheres are getting mixed. In activities of an outwardly serious nature hides an element of play. Recognized play, on the other hand, is no longer able to maintain its true play character as a result of being taken too seriously and being technically over-organized. The indispensable qualities of detachment, artlessness and gladness are thus lost.'

It is exactly the same with cricket.

The feeling has been reinforced by the shift of the financial nerve centre of the game to the subcontinent, and the staggering sums of money at stake these days. The arrival of satellite TV widened the reach of the game in India like never before. Giant corporations, sensing the new opportunity and the new audience that was making vastly keener and more aggressive India's original passion for cricket, moved in with their fat wallets.

From the 1990s, as satellite TV began to penetrate wider and deeper into Indian society, cricket on the subcontinent began to exponentially increase the amount of money it generated from advertisements and TV rights. Billboards of Indian companies began to be seen in tournaments played outside India. It made perfect sense for the big companies. The number of viewers was shooting up, and Indians, sitting in India, were watching, for instance, India versus England at Headingley. By advertising there, through satellite TV, you were getting as many eyeballs as you wanted of consumers in India.

By the time the World Cup in England came around in 1999, several of the main sponsors—Hero Honda, Pepsi, LG—were targeting subcontinental audiences. Along with its heart and soul, the game's money muscle had swapped homes. Now, towards the end of the first decade of the twenty-first century, India has become the key to the financial health of the game, to its very well being.

Today, India controls more than 70 per cent of cricket's global revenues. TV advertising spots of a few seconds between overs sell for thousands of dollars. After furious bidding, global media rights for international cricket in India between March 2006 and March 2010 were sold for US$612 million. Last year Nike won the five-year rights to sponsor the Indian cricket team's official kit for US$43 million. And a TV company spent six times as much as India did for the moon mission, Chandrayan, for the rights to telecast the inaugural season of the Indian Premier League Twenty20 championship in 2008.

Many of the Australian players make a lot of their money from endorsement deals in India. And the US$550 million that the ICC received for sponsorship and broadcast rights to the 2003 and 2007 World Cups and three Champions Trophies would not have been possible without the advertising and satellite-TV money from the subcontinent.

In February 2008, at a luxury hotel in south Mumbai, the auction for players to take part in the first season of the IPL league in April took place.

The proceedings (which married Bollywood stars, industry captains and cricketers in a glamorous, cash-rich wedding) overwhelmed the TV channels and the front pages of papers. Players' services for forty-four days of Twenty20 cricket between teams that comprised Indian and international players were auctioned to the highest bidder. Each bidder was a franchisee of a team, something like a club owner in European football.

Mahendra Singh Dhoni's services were bought for US$1.5million, and several other rising Indian players like young Ishant Sharma and Rohit Sharma were assured of the sort of money they could scarcely have dreamt of twelve months ago.

The Indian board came out of all this rather well. Within days of the auction—and with the season yet to begin—the board had earned US$723 million through franchisee rights (that is, the money gleaned from individuals in exchange of the rights to become franchisee of a particular team) and US$5 million via title sponsorship rights. A chunk of that US$723 million will be distributed to the cricket boards of countries from which players will participate in the league.

It's hardly odd that other cricket boards (and the ICC) hold the Indian board as much in awe as in fear.

We saw that most recently after the affair involving Harbhajan and Symonds in Sydney in

January 2008. India lost the Test after a string of shocking umpiring blunders. India was right to have felt robbed; there were eight crucial decisions that went against the team. India then asked that Steve Bucknor, the particularly guilty umpire, not stand in the subsequent Test—something unprecedented for a team to ask for from cricket's international governing body.

It worked. But it was India's financial clout that allowed its cricket board to arm-twist the ICC into sacking Bucknor for the subsequent Test in Perth.

Divorced from the context, though, the removal of Bucknor was a good thing. If players can be dropped for not playing well, why not officials who often hold their futures in their hands? It has happened in football, and it is high time that it did in cricket. International cricket is a highly organized business. There is no place for incompetence in corporations.

But that isn't the point here. The point is that India could do it because it holds the purse strings of international cricket. It got away with bullying the ICC earlier (in South Africa in 2001) and it will again. Money doesn't merely talk. It screams so loud that it silences any opposition.

When India asked for Bucknor's removal, the ICC boss, Malcolm Speed, gave in because it was the most expedient way to hold the tour together.

(He didn't of course admit to the fact that he had yielded.) The financial and political implications of India pulling out of the tour—and its subsequent fallout—in terms of the future of the game were too enormous to gamble with, or even to contemplate.

Several former cricketers have made this point, though few as strongly as former Australia captain Allan Border. 'They [India] have probably too much say in matters even though it's a global game,' Border told an Australian paper in February 2008.

A lot of us, though, can't get enough of India's financial muscle in the world of cricket—and the frequent flexing of it. It's a small world when it comes to cricket, but here is at least one thing in which we are dictating terms to the rest of the world. At least off the field.

Here, too, as in the matter of Twenty20, I am a little anachronistic. I think that sort of thinking is too misguidedly jingoistic to afford any comfort or pleasure. Besides, if the wheel were to turn—and it usually does—and the balance of financial power one day shifts away from India, there will be others more than willing to do to India what India is doing to them now.

And on the field? Well, at least we aren't doing too badly there either. In November 2008 India beat Australia, (then) the best team in the world, 2–0 in a

Test series at home. This was the most crushing loss Australia has suffered in the past twenty-five years.

In 2008, India beat England in a series away from home—the first occasion it did so since 1986. It returned, before that, from a magnificent, memorable tour of Australia, where—led with remarkable gumption by Kumble in the Tests and Dhoni in the one-days—it would be cornered but not written off. And if it lost the Test series against Sri Lanka after winning in England, it won the one-day series against the Lankans right after that—something they had not managed to do away from home ever before.

At the moment, India is looking to have a serious shot at becoming the best team in the world in both Tests and one-day internationals; and it has decimated the fifty-over world champions in the last one-day international series, thumping the Aussies twice within four days in January 2008. Australia is no longer the best team in the world. And India, Sri Lanka and South Africa are in the hunt for that title.

Not bad for a country that took more than three decades to win its first international match away from home.

Unsurprisingly, we have appropriated cricket for ourselves: it is our game. It belongs to us (and, we often think, only us) as much as we belong to it. Three decades ago, I—or hundreds of thousands of little boys growing up in a city in India, besotted with the game, in the throes of their heightening passion gradually transforming into a lifelong affair—considered any cricket played on the subcontinent as an approximation of the real thing. *That* happened on English cricket grounds. A seven-year-old in Delhi or Bangalore today believes that the game played on his home ground is the genuine stuff; all else is a diluted version.

The manner in which India has made cricket its very own—in terms of the money it generates, the frenzy it engenders and its intrusion into every aspect of public life, from pop culture to politics—is a signifier of India's post-colonial present and its newfound, post-globalized poise and confidence.

Like the English language, cricket was a game made popular in India by the British. And like the English language, Indians have over the years appropriated it in a very Indian way.

It is not merely that cricket touches more hearts in India than in the land of its birth; the pitch and tenor of the unbridled enthusiasm India has for it is very different from what you see in, say, England or Australia or New Zealand or South Africa.

At grounds in those countries too, the tricolour flies high nowadays. The din and the excitement and the passion that we associate with cricket played in India has infiltrated foreign grounds. Those qualities have been gradually brought in over there somewhat by the swelling number of the diaspora. But they have become a part of the texture of the atmosphere largely because of the many Indians who now travel abroad to watch the cricket.

When I started watching cricket in the 1970s, you couldn't have imagined Indian fans travelling to the Caribbean to watch India play. But with disposable incomes rising and foreign travel becoming as easy, frequent and unremarkable as travelling from, say, Delhi to Jaipur, Indians—or at any rate a certain class of Indians—are going, in large numbers, to watch their team play in foreign countries.

Lawrence Booth, one of England's wittier cricket writers, describes these fans in his book, *Cricket, Lovely Cricket?*: 'One of the strangest parts of being in the Caribbean for the World Cup in 2007 was the sight of middle-aged Indian men hanging around hotel lobbies as they wondered what to do with their day—beach or, er, beach?—following India's early exit. The rooms had been booked well in advance in expectation of India's involvement in the Super Eights, but their team had not obliged. Yet here they were, wearing the middle-class cricket fan's touring costume of choice: polo shirt, fashionably long Bermuda shorts, expensive flip-flops, shades perched extraneously on their head. . . Indians had the money and they were starting to put it to good use.'

So there you go. Cricket as a badge of national identity, as an industry, as an inclusive pop cultural pursuit, as a reflection of the patterns of consumerist spending among the flourishing, urban elite: Whether we like it or not, this game has moved from the margins to the centre of our lives. It flows into and colours areas of our existence with which we had once believed it had little to do.

The
Premier
Confrontation

It is always rash to speak of a reinvention and renaissance after a terrific Test series and one gloriously triumphant one-day series—just as it is stupid to speak of desolation and hopelessness after one defeat—but there did seem to be something swirling in the air of the Australian summer of 2007–08. It was to do with the things we saw in this Indian side that we have seen but very rarely. A new poise, a new self-assuredness, a new courage and confidence. (In a way, that is of a piece with the India we have seen in this new century, the India that was forged on the anvil of Sourav Ganguly's fearless leadership. We shall get to that later.)

I am aware that you might ask why this book alludes more to games versus Australia than other teams. That's because India has shown the character that fans want of it when it has played Australia.

Most of our greatest victories in the modern era (some of our greatest triumphs *ever*) have come in the past eight years or so against Australia, the undisputed champions of the world in that period.

Think of Eden Gardens in 2001; of Adelaide in 2003; of Perth in 2008; and Mohali and Nagpur later on in the same year.

Several of our modern cricketing legends—Rahul Dravid, V.V.S. Laxman and Sachin Tendulkar—seem to reserve their very best for that side; they have, when faced with contemporary cricket's toughest opposition, given us innings and memories we are likely to never forget.

Have a look at these facts: Six of VVS's thirteen Test hundreds have come against Australia. Both Tendulkar and VVS have more than 2000 Test runs against Australia. Tendulkar has scored ten hundreds in Tests against Australia—more than any batsman in the modern game. On only three occasions in the past fifteen years has Australia conceded more than 600 runs in an innings; on all three occasions, it has been against India. Australia has lost more Tests to India—seven—than to any other international side in this century. And when India beat Australia 2–0 at home in the autumn of 2008, it was the worst defeat the Aussies have suffered in a quarter century since losing 0–3 to the West Indies in 1983 (a time when the Caribbeans were the best side in the world).

It is a tribute to the quality of cricket India has consistently played against the team that lorded over world cricket for fifteen years that the premier, most-awaited confrontation in world cricket between 2001 and 2009 was neither England and Australia nor India and Pakistan; it was between India and Australia. Till Australia fell off their perch in the second half of 2009, India v Australia was the real deal; it was the unambiguous classic of contemporary cricket.

Australia, in the autumn of 2008, was still the leader in world cricket. But the fact that they were hanging on to that title only by a thread exemplifies how gloriously India had challenged the champions in recent times.

To return to that tour of 2007-08.

With the acrimonious, bitterly fought Test series over and the one-day series yet to begin, Australia captain Ricky Ponting had said that the best-of-three finals would not need to run their course; it would take merely two games to settle matters.

In the event, it did. India had won two in a row.

At the post-match press conference, looking dazed if not exactly confused (he did unequivocally say that his team had been outplayed by India in both matches), his face pinched and drawn, Ponting must have been regretting having made that prediction. A born-again betting man once known to be partial to greyhound racing, he should have known better than to tempt fate. Or cricket.

But then, who could have bet on India? Who

could have really hoped that things would have turned out quite this way?

The story of that tour is not merely that of the one-day series and the Test encounter that preceded it. *Real* cricket fans are great ones for going further back, of burrowing into the mass of events and statistics and games to find a *pattern*. We love cause–effect, you see, we are big on progression. Given that we consider Test cricket to be the most challenging, most enjoyable version of the game that we so adore, we have *five days* to ruminate over things during a match.

Can you blame us?

So where it all began, this needle between India and Australia on the cricket field, was at the Eden Gardens in Kolkata on a balmy spring day in March 2001. India was at the time led by Sourav Ganguly— brash, outspoken, India's most atypical Test captain ever. He was a hustler and a streetfighter, who gave back as good as he got.

Well up on Australia captain Steve Waugh's theory of 'mental disintegration' (otherwise known as sledging), Ganguly had kept Waugh waiting for the toss—an act of calculated disrespect and impoliteness that let the Australians know where they stood, no bowing, no scraping—during the first Test of the series in Mumbai.

The team did not walk the captain's talk. Australia

won in Mumbai, scarcely breaking sweat. They had, with that win, taken their tally of consecutive Test victories to sixteen. No one had come close in the 124 years that Test cricket had been played. By the time the teams arrived in Kolkata, Waugh was talking about breaching the 'final frontier'—a series win against India in India, something that no Australian side had managed since 1969.

By the end of the third day's play in Kolkata, that appeared a formality. India seemed dead and buried. And then came VVS and Dravid. VVS scored 281, Dravid 180, and India—improbably, unprecedentedly—had turned the match on its head.

Australia lost that Test, and then the series. Waugh's final frontier remained unbreached. He was to retire soon. His swansong was a series in Australia in December–January 2003–04. His opponents? India.

In that series, on which rested Waugh's legacy, Ganguly's India looked Australia in the eye and refused to blink. India drew the Test series 1–1 (an utterly rare thing for a team visiting Australia), and Waugh spent his last day in international cricket trying to avert a series defeat.

'Ever so rarely comes a series that marks a turning point in history,' cricket's bible, the *Wisden Almanack* noted with characteristic grace and precision afterwards. 'It may be years or decades before the significance of India's tour of Australia in 2003–04 can be truly assessed, but in this series they announced themselves as a force in Test cricket, after years of living on promise and vain dazzle. They didn't quite end Australia's reign, but how close they came.'

India v Australia had become world cricket's marquee showdown. The series started being called the greatest in the modern era, a genuine, much-deserved sobriquet in the exaggerated world of platitude-filled cricket reporting.

Australia did actually breach the final frontier: they beat India in a Test series in India when they toured in the autumn of 2004. They won the series 2–1; India pulled off a victory in a dead rubber on a dustbowl of a pitch in Mumbai.

India's tour of 2007–08 was in this backdrop— one of intense rivalry, immense talent and extreme competitiveness.

India lost the series (it was denied in Sydney by eight outrageous umpiring decisions) but it did something unique: it won, thrillingly, remarkably, a Test at Perth—one of the fastest wickets in the world and a venue at which it was not expected to last the full course of the match.

There was something else in Perth. As in Kolkata seven years ago, Dravid and VVS made significant contributions (if not half as staggering as the ones they had made then). And India halted Australia's winning streak of sixteen consecutive Tests. Waugh, then. Ponting, now. Same opposition. Such symmetry. We fans thrive on these patterns, didn't I tell you?

Perth sent out a clear statement of intent. This team would not be cowed. And if it could manage to get its foot on the neck of the world's finest side (and also, some say, its greatest bully and most graceless loser), it would not let up till its opponents had choked.

You could see that intent—and that frisson— every time Harbhajan picked up the wicket of Symonds or Hayden (the man who had called him an 'obnoxious weed' before the one-day series). You could see it in Tendulkar's murderous century in the first final. You could see it in young Ishant Sharma's eyes as he ran in full tilt, his long hair in his slipstream, bowling fast enough and accurately enough to repeatedly work Ponting over. (And there is the other, important thing. In Ishant and Dhoni, Gautam Gambhir and Rohit Sharma, we glimpsed the men who would be our future stars.)

India badly wanted to beat Australia at Perth, but then, we are all terribly good at badly wanting things. Whether we get them depends not merely on desire but on ability and wherewithal; it depends on how big a heart one has, and how large a stomach for a fight.

We saw that again when Australia came to India later that year.

Kumble retired from Test cricket in the middle of that series. Led with imagination and tact by Dhoni, powered as much by vintage batting from Ganguly, VVS and Tendulkar as superb bowling from young Ishant and newcomer leg-spinner Amit Mishra, India humiliated Australia by 320 runs in the second Test in Mohali and finished the series off in Nagpur, winning by 172 runs.

It was heady stuff, not merely because of the result, nor merely because it took India to the Number Two spot in the ICC Test rankings, nor because it stripped from Australia the cloak of invincibility, leaving it vulnerable and exposed in the muggy Indian autumn. It was magnificent because it was the sort of *symmetrical* triumph we fans so adore. The 2–0 win at home against Australia was especially delightful because it was so well rounded an achievement, dovetailing the glory of the past and informed with suggestions of what the legacy of that past might be and, therefore, what the future might hold for us.

The magic of triumph married to the miracle of a seamless transition: What more could we have asked for, really?

It doesn't get better than this, Dhoni said after the limited-overs final in Australia early in 2008. Well, I don't know about that. Fans simply can't get enough. Some of us will ask: why are *we* not the top side in the world? Shouldn't we *be*? Haven't we waited *long enough*?

But we are all agreed upon one thing. We shall continue to run the images of India v Australia games over and over in our minds. And, however many years from now it may be, we shall *still* tear ourselves away from whatever it is that we might be doing when the re-re-run of some unforgettable game turns up on TV.

'Remember Eden Gardens in 2001? Adelaide in 2004? Perth in 2008? Mohali? Nagpur?' we shall ask each other and ourselves, our faces aglow with remembered delight.

Will it last, this run? Can it? Who can tell?

By the time this book is published, the story would have moved on. That's the fun of writing about this sort of thing. That's the trouble with it.

Either way, there is one thing that is indisputable: Cricket is the only team game at which we really are any good. Who is to blame if it is then the only team game in which we are remotely interested?

For us, nothing ever will become the new cricket. If there is ever to be something like that, it will have to be some version of the game as we know it now.

Ask yourself this. Just how much spectator interest has shooting generated after Abhinav Bindra became the first Indian to win an individual Olympic gold at Beijing in 2008? Are people hurrying home to watch amateur boxing on TV after our medals in Beijing? Is there a frenzied interest in billiards after Pankaj Advani became world champion?

A quick pop quiz: India won an international football tournament in late 2007. We did, again, in 2009. Whom did we beat? Where was it played? Scores, anyone? Answers on a postcard please.

The covenant between a team and its fans is inviolable, sacrosanct. We can never bear to not follow our side when it plays. This comes with its inevitable disappointment and misery but our allegiance remains unbroken. It is not like the colas or the cars or the credit cars or the insurance policies the players endorse. Don't like it? Flush it down the toilet. Sell it off. Exchange it for something better. Buy a new one.

When things go wrong on the pitch, some of us go on mock funeral processions. Some of us burn effigies. Both gestures are as banal as they are despicable. But none of us can stay away. (Not being able to stay away is in the nature of addiction, which always has irrationality at its heart.) Had we been able to, TV ratings would slip and channels wouldn't pay millions for satellite rights and companies wouldn't put their money where the nation's heart isn't. The fact that they do suggests that there are many millions of us out there.

All of us think we have a stake in the Indian cricket team. We have invested our emotions, our passions, our frenzy, our whole *lives* in following this side. There is simply too much riding on those eleven men, we believe. The Indian cricket team is for us like a giant corporation. How its stocks rise and fall has a bearing on our lives.

We can't support another team. We can't be bothered to care half as much about any other game. It's either this or nothing. And nothing is so much worse.

I have always wondered why the average Indian does not carry such strong feelings over into other walks of life. We make so much of one defeat on a cricket field that we ask for the captain to be sacked and denounce our players as wimps and threaten to attack their families. But we don't ask for our politicians to be hanged and quartered for corruption, we shrug and make do when the roads in our cities are disgraceful, when we see—especially after having returned from our trips abroad—how shameful our public transport is . . .

Why is it that we don't protest? Why do we reserve our outrage for the cricket?

My guess is this: we can't allow our players to slip—it would be too much of a blow to our sense of self-worth.

That
Life,
That
Fame,
Will
Be
His

That

Life,

That

Fame,

Will

Be

His.

Our obsession with the game is not merely to do with fandom. Never mind which social class or region they come from, many of cricket's devotees in India passionately believe that they one day will become the stars others will watch. This conviction has been strengthened by the fact that game has opened up; it is no longer the bastion of a particular social class or region.

How many cricketers does Mumbai—once the crucible of Indian cricket—have in the national team now? How many players from the middle or upper middle classes? It doesn't matter any longer.

Sourav Ganguly, India's most successful captain ever, comes from Bengal—a state without a tradition of producing cricket players of note. Dhoni, the man in whom we are investing our hopes for the future, is the son of a railway ticket collector from Jharkhand—a young state without a tradition of producing, well, anything respectable. Irfan Pathan is the son of a muezzin in Baroda. Virender Sehwag is from Najafgarh, a place not many Indians knew existed before he exploded into international cricket. R.P. Singh's father has a modest job with Indian Telephones in Rae Bareili. Praveen Kumar, the man of the match in India's unforgettable one-day triumph against Australia in Brisbane in March 2008, is from a family of wrestlers in Meerut.

They have turned cricket into the new meritocracy. Everyone is invited.

Thanks to the IPL, Dhoni earned about US$1.25 million in a very short season of neither terribly demanding nor intense play in a form of cricket not even Twenty20's most ardent admirers will consider the premier form of the game. A Delhi University professor, in comparison, the *Times of India* calculated, will earn one-third that amount over a career of thirty-five years.

All this has happened in a country called New India, which seems to be rather different from the India we knew and grew up in. Here (a place where we have reinvented the language to turn an adjective into a proper noun), money—and its visible manifestations—is good; it is power in a way it wasn't ever before. And we need it, need more of it, and the ways in which it can be acquired hold for us a sort of talismanic value. (This is neither a good thing nor a bad thing. It is just how things *are*.)

In a way, of course, the evolution of the new meritocracy—as so much else—began with Sachin Tendulkar.

Now take a deep breath. And think about this.

When Tendulkar first played for India in November 1989, the Babri Masjid was intact; the Berlin Wall had just about fallen; Margaret Thatcher was prime minister of the UK; Nirvana was two years away from recording *Smells Like Teen Spirit*; Steffi Graf was Wimbledon champion; and India had neither mobile phones nor the Internet.

That is how long he has been around. Long enough for the world to have changed beyond recognition.

Think about this again. What was *your* life like in 1989? Tendulkar—prodigious, peerless, generation-straddling poster boy of a sport that defines the world's most populous democracy—is still at it, doing what he used to twenty years ago.

Small wonder then that an entire nation should be so much in his thrall.

For close to two decades, Tendulkar has dominated India's collective consciousness in a way no other sportsperson (well, no other *person*) has. He has more than bound a nation. He has bridged the generation gap.

Remember that ad in which a grandmother was seen praying for his success, her rosary beads clattering to the floor as Tendulkar smashed one out of the ground? Well, grandmothers *do* love him.

And fathers and sons are united for once—in

their devotion to him. When Tendulkar bats against Pakistan, Ramachandra Guha tells us *In a Corner of a Foreign Field*, India's television audience exceeds the population of Europe.

If Sourav Ganguly was Indian cricket's Rolling Stones—iconoclastic, snarling, sneering, getting up the opposition's nose—Tendulkar is our Beatles—universally loved and lovable.

Longevity, of course, is merely one of the reasons for the sort of hold Tendulkar has over us. What he has done in those twenty years is another: he has dominated his sport in a manner no other Indian—and almost no other sportsperson in the world—has ever done.

It is convenient to get the facts out of the way first. Tendulkar has already made forty-two centuries in 159 Test matches; he has scored 12,773 runs; he has forty-three hundreds in 425 one-day internationals; in them, he has made 16,684 runs at the rate of 86 scored for every 100 balls faced. (Just try scoring eighty-five hundreds—the number of international centuries Tendulkar has made—while playing with your child in your living room. You are likely to find it terribly hard.) And he would have left these figures behind by the time you hold this book in your hands.

In October 2008, in a Test against Australia at Mohali, he broke Brian Lara's record to become the man who has scored more runs than anyone else in Test cricket history. In the innings in which he reached the landmark—an uninhibited, almost flawless innings—he was out for 88.

We groaned with disappointment. He didn't get a hundred, did he? He ought to have. Whatever he gives us, what we want from his is always, unfairly, that much more. It's inhuman, the burden of expectation the man has had to shoulder.

It is worthwhile saying it in an unambiguous sentence: Tendulkar has made more runs and more centuries than any other cricketer in the history of international cricket. He is, as *Wisden* calls him, the 'most wholesome' cricketer of the modern era.

He is now thirty-five years old. The story is by no means over.

But the statistics are not the whole story either. Tendulkar is unarguably the most successful Indian cricketer ever, but merely the success does not explain the adulation that he continues to inspire.

In a way, his career—and the tale of how he acquired his frenzied, worshipping masses of admirers—has something to do with *when* he came along, and how his life became entwined with contemporary India's story of growth, hope and change, and its recent and desperate need for self-congratulation and chest-thumping.

As always with Tendulkar, timing is critical. And he could not have chosen to arrive in international cricket at a more appropriate moment. The protectionist economy was being opened up, and India was beginning its journey towards becoming a global economic powerhouse.

'Greed,' Gordon Gekko told us in Oliver Stone's 1987 film, *Wall Street*, 'is good.' It wasn't, not yet in India, not quite, when Tendulkar made his debut, but over the course of his remarkable career, it would get there. Or at least being wealthy, outrageously wealthy, and not apologetic about it, would become acceptable as India sloughed off its old diffidence about money and ostentation.

When he appeared, India was beginning to give birth to a new, affluent, urban middle class. Tendulkar, sixteen years old then, more boy than man, exceptionally gifted and incredibly mature for his age, very quickly began to embody all the qualities that this new class treasured.

He was a world-beater, a global citizen; he was smart, he dressed well, he drove sexy cars; he was, above all, a self-made man. And the money he earned: huge sums, unthinkable ones, more than anyone had ever made before him. He was Indian sport's first global brand.

As cultural critic and author Mike Marqusee has suggested in an essay in *Wisden Asia Cricket*: 'The intensity of the Tendulkar cult is about much more than just cricket. Unwittingly and unwillingly, he has found himself at the epicentre of a rapidly evolving popular culture shaped by the intertwined growth of a consumerist middle class and an increasingly aggressive form of national identity. National aspirations and national frustrations are poured by millions into his every performance.'

And yet he appears to exemplify certain cherished Indian values: humility, deference to elders, and a zealously guarded private life. Respect for all the things that ought to be respected. With Tendulkar, we can have it both ways, and are delighted about that: he typifies the best of both worlds that we think we strive to inhabit.

And what of the play?

In that, too, we have got the best of both worlds from Tendulkar. On the field, he is safe as houses; yet he is as destructive as a battle tank. He is a fantasy combination of Sunil Gavaskar and Viv Richards.

His defence is textbook perfect; so is his attack. His inventiveness and improvization according to the pitch and the state of the game have left us breathless again and again. And he was the first Indian batsman who could score mountains of runs, and score them with a sort of murderous intent. What could we do but worship him?

I shouldn't really get started on the sporting memories he has given me: the blitzkrieg of a century on a brutally quick Perth pitch when he was nineteen years old; the century in Bloemfontein in South Africa in 2001 when he turned the spooned shot over third man into a potent, attacking stroke; the innings amid the dust storm in Sharjah against Australia; that plunder against Pakistan in the 2003 World Cup.

No, no, the list is too long, and it is pointless to go on.

It is probably simpler to go back to a few numbers. He has scored twenty-four Test hundreds away from home—always the true test of class for an international player. And, just to give you a sense of how much he had achieved so unbelievably early, he had scored six hundreds in four countries by the time he was nineteen years old.

But Tendulkar isn't nineteen years old any longer. That is something we tend to seem to forget. He was once the son that every father wanted. Now, with two grown children of his own, he is the father that every son or daughter would rather have. His iconography has appropriately changed. So has the brand positioning (he now endorses life insurance), but the cachet remains unaltered.

It would have been stupid to have expected his game to not have altered as he has got older, as his body has become weary and has slowed down, and the opposition has had more and more of a chance to study, analyse and dissect his game and make plans for him.

Tendulkar has adapted. And often adapted when the going has not been good. It took him eighteen months (from April 2004 to December 2005) to go from Century Number Thirty-three to Century Number Thirty-five, but he did get there. And well beyond.

He endured 2003, his, injury-hit, worst year in international cricket, in which he scored 153 runs in five Tests at an average of 17. (His career average still stands at 54.) Coming off that year, in January 2004 against Australia in Sydney, he scored 241 not out: an unlovely innings of awesome rigour and concentration, shrinking his repertoire by refusing to play at all the shot that had got him out previously.

He showed us, that if he *really* put his mind to it, he simply would not be dismissed.

It was monumental. It was riveting.

'At Sydney, I just decided when I walked out to bat that I wasn't going to get out,' he told *wisden.com* afterwards. 'No matter how long I batted, I wasn't going to get out.'

He didn't actually, remaining not out on 60 in the second innings.

That resolve to hang in there and accumulate

runs sounded unfamiliar to us. But the self-confidence that allows a batsman to make a promise like that to himself—and to keep it—did not. That was *very* like Tendulkar.

That is the sort of response to crises that the man has shown in the autumn of his extraordinary career. He takes fewer risks now; at the same time, he is harder to get out once he gets going. (In 2004, for instance, his smallest hundred was 194 not out.)

It is this dogged, grimly determined Tendulkar that some of his fans seem to mind. He has compromised swashbuckle for solidity. He has gone from being hunter to gatherer.

Even nowadays, when he opens his shoulders and loses his wary watchfulness, he can show us the beautiful savagery that we associated with him of old. Yet we tend to sometimes regret the fact that the sense of thrilling possibility that he once brought with him to the crease no longer hovers in the air when he comes out to bat.

Tendulkar is playing for records, some of his detractors love to say. I don't think that's true. I think Tendulkar is playing a low-risk game that will give him—and, often, his team—maximum benefit at this stage of his career.

The comparison with one of Tendulkar's idols, Richards, has been made over and over again. Richards never changed, he never tempered his savagery. But, as Sambit Bal explains in an essay on Cricinfo: 'His last three years fetched Richards only 978 runs, from nineteen Tests, at an average of 36.22, with only one century. Richards was too proud to defend, but he was a lesser player for it during his last years.'

It is hard to tell how long Tendulkar will go on. Certainly, it is just as hard to imagine cricket without Tendulkar as it is to imagine Tendulkar without cricket.

Here is another staggering fact: he has spent more years of his life playing international cricket than he has not. (And he yet retains, people close to him say, the inimitable, indefatigable quality that coaches and seniors found so endearing in him when he was a teenager: he still just loves to bat and bat.)

It strikes me that there is a whole generation of Indian cricket fans who are, say, in their mid- or late-twenties, recall no Indian cricket other than that dominated by Tendulkar. They will, once he goes, realize the strangeness of not having him there. They will have to deal with the awful vacuum. And they shall speak to future generations of what it was like to have him around.

We do know this, all of us: we shall not see the likes of him. Ever again.

And what of fans like me, the ones slouching towards forty, the ones who had cricketing heroes like Gundappa Viswanath and Kapil Dev before Tendulkar burst on to our consciousness and the world's?

'I believe that heroes,' wrote the poet, critic and cricket fan, Alan Ross, 'are necessary to children and that as we grow up it becomes more difficult to establish them in the increasingly unresponsive soil of our individual mythology. Occasionally, the adult imagination is caught and sometimes it is held; but the image rarely takes root.'

Tendulkar's magic has been that his image *has* taken root in the adult imagination. He was the first sporting hero I had who was younger than me. When he first played, he was sixteen, and I twenty.

He has made men past adolescence discover again the joys of hero worship. Even the cynics amongst us, those of us ever wary of idolatry, become like awed, star-struck children when he is at the crease. God (if there was one, we think), on a good day, would do well to match his genius.

As our lives grow more complicated and burdensome, Tendulkar—piercing four men on the off side with that breathtaking cover drive—shows us that sudden, heart-lurching delirium still has a place in our lives.

When he takes guard, our stomachs churn, and our hands feel clammy. Even those of us who believe in neither a god nor a devil find ourselves praying (to whom exactly?) that he sticks around long enough to give us an innings (*another* one) to cherish.

Here is Ross again. 'Heroes die with one's youth. They are pinned like butterflies to the setting board of early memories.' Far more effectively than cosmetic surgery, Tendulkar has made us all young again.

Without Tendulkar, there would have been no Dhoni or Yuvraj Singh or any other Indian cricketer as global brands; had he not been such a success, the allure of cricket as a life-transforming career would not have been so well defined, and the dream of that alchemy would not have been dreamt by hundreds of thousands of young men across India today.

As it turns out, they do dream—on the Maidan in Kolkata, in Shivaji Park in Mumbai, on the barren fields in the wastelands of Bihar, in posh cricket academies all over the country. The boy with his state-of-the-art kit in an affluent, urban family believes he can emulate his heroes, that *that* life, that fame, can be, *will* be his, with as much fervour as the boy in a dot of a village with his makeshift stumps and inadequate gear.

What does it take, they ask themselves, just *what*?

Talent, rigour and a lucky break. Look at Pathan. Look at Joginder. Look at Praveen, at Ishant, at RP, at Sehwag. Look at Dhoni.

If they can, why not me?

Only a select few break through to that stratosphere. Perhaps even they are aware of how slim the chances are. But that in no way dilutes the intensity of their desire. For is that not the stuff dreams are made of?

We'll
Miss
You
So
Much

The Fab Five are no more. I mean, they are still fab, of course (they always will be); but there aren't five of them playing together for India any longer.

Sachin Tendulkar, Rahul Dravid, Sourav Ganguly, V.V.S. Laxman and Anil Kumble have been the pillars (and the superstructure) of India's most glorious cricketing triumphs. As Peter Roebuck wrote in an essay on cricinfo.com: 'If Kumble was the colossus, Sachin Tendulkar the champion, Rahul Dravid the craftsman, V.V.S. Laxman the sorcerer, then Ganguly was the inspiration.'

If we take the beginning of this century (and the time that Ganguly, then Dravid, and then Kumble led India in Tests) as the sort of starting point when all five—or at least more than one of them—were firing away at the same time, India's performance underwent a dramatic transformation. It's worthwhile to measure it by the success rate in Tests overseas—for my money, the truest, most genuine indicator of achievement.

India started playing international cricket in 1932.

In the sixty-eight years between 1932 and 2000, India won thirteen Tests away from home. Ganguly became Test captain in November 2000. In the eight years between then and November 2008, we have won eighteen Tests playing abroad.

You tell me what that might suggest.

In these years, India has gone from being a team that terrorized opponents at home on designer, turning tracks and were, largely, wimps when it toured, to a formidable side that has won games across the world (in England, the West Indies, Australia, South Africa, Pakistan), playing with a toughness and a confidence that is invigorating, thrilling and often impossible to believe for fans who grew up following Indian cricket in the 1970s, 1980s or 1990s.

In the way that makes sport so worthwhile and entertaining, the whole of the Fab Five has been greater than the sum of their parts.

But what they meant, these five men, isn't merely in the numbers. (The numbers are staggering: the runs they have made, the wickets they have taken, the matches they have saved, turned around, and won.) What is it that they have given us fans over so many years?

I won't get started on Tendulkar again. What of the remaining Fab Four?

Anil Kumble (International Debut: April 1990)

Over December and January 2003–04 in Australia, Anil Kumble—his reputation as a bowler away from the subcontinent having been chipped away at for years by critics who couldn't see beyond their noses—rediscovered himself. He proved to his detractors what ought to have been blindingly obvious many years ago: he was India's most committed, no-nonsense, selfless bowler in any condition.

In that Australian summer, in what was then being described as the greatest series in the modern game (and one notable, for most of us, for India's magnificent batting triumphs), Kumble took twenty-four wickets in three Tests.

In the final Test at Sydney, as batsmen ran bowlers into the ground (India, for instance, scored 916 runs over two innings and lost only nine wickets, and Australia did almost as well too), Kumble ran in with that look of grim, unwavering concentration on his face, bent his back, and picked up twelve wickets. He bowled eighty-eight overs and five balls in the match.

And all some of us tend to talk about was Tendulkar's 241 not out in the first innings.

That series was a sort of second coming for Kumble. He missed the epochal, epic 2001 series against Australia at home. Harbhajan Singh stepped in, stepped up, and was discovered as a match-winner. From then on, whenever India needed to play a single spinner, Kumble's place in the side was at stake. He was dropped for almost the entire duration of the 2003 World Cup campaign in South Africa. He got a look-in in Australia because Harbhajan, this time, was out with injury. (Oh, the patterns, didn't I tell you earlier?) And he grasped the chance he got—as he always did—with both hands.

It didn't seem odd to those of us who have followed Kumble's career with a mixture of reverential fascination and frustration. (The frustration is born of the fact that not everybody has been as reverential of or fascinated by the man's monumental effort.) We thought, that day, of Kumble against the West Indies in Antigua in 2002. While batting, he had had his jaw fractured by Mervyn Dillon. Against everybody's advice—and to everybody's consternation—he came on to bowl. Wrapped in white gauze and armoured with his inimitable grit and resolve, he toiled away for fourteen overs. Oh, and he took Brian Lara's wicket.

It was all pretty much uphill from that series to nearly the end of Kumble's career in the autumn of 2008. He went out, as he always loved to say, on his own terms. At the age of thirty-eight, his body could not take the toll of the game any longer, he said. He had had one poor series against Sri Lanka; he seemed a shadow of the bowler he used to be against the Australians when they came to India. And so, after one final caught and bowled dismissal against the old enemy, bowling with the webbing in his hand split, he said, in the middle of the series, that it was all over. His powers were dwindling, his body would not go where his mind wanted to, and Kumble knew it was time. Typical again.

He finished as the third highest wicket taker in the history of Test cricket. He has so many more wickets than any other Indian bowler that it seems improbable now that anyone will catch up. And he became India's Test captain (a job both Dravid and Tendulkar declined at the time and Dhoni was seen to be too raw for) in the twilight of his glittering career.

Kumble knew exactly why he had been offered the captaincy. But he made no fuss, he said yes to the job just the way he had said yes to anything that had been thrown at him all through his cricketing life.

The dignity and quiet grace with which he took it on, his conduct and composure, were of a piece with his style of bowling. Shane Warne had leg breaks that ripped in and kicked off the pitch, that turned at so precise right angles that you could use a setsquare to measure them. Mutthiah Muralitharan had the guile of the doosra to add to the frightening, vicious spin he extracted from the wicket.

Kumble was never a great turner of the ball. He had the topspinner—the nearly straight ball that befuddled generations of batsmen—and he picked up the googly and remarkable variations of pace in the later stages of his career. If Kumble is to be compared to a fellow bowler, it is not to the spin wizards in the history of the game; the analogy ought to be with the great Australian fast bowler, Glenn McGrath—just as nagging, just as metronomically accurate, the Maestro of Millimetres.

The way in which Kumble performed perhaps especially on the final day of his career in Delhi in November 2008 offered a sort of coda to his entire career: with gentle heroism, unstinting commitment and silent, ceaseless endeavour.

Sourav Ganguly (International Debut: January 1992; *Real* International Debut: June 1996)

I watched Sourav Ganguly's penultimate Test innings on TV at my—and his—hometown, Kolkata. The match was against Australia, in Nagpur. The public discourse in Kolkata in clubs, bars and street corners (sorry, that may not be a fabulously representative sample, but those are the places I tend to hang out at when I go to Kolkata on my annual visits) was dominated by the former captain and his decision to quit. Was he pushed? Should he have? Couldn't he have played for a little while longer? Oh, Dada!

Hell, the largest-selling Bengali daily put Ganguly in as part of the headline the day Sachin Tendulkar got his fortieth Test hundred. (Ganguly was 27 not out at stumps.) And on his final day in Test cricket, after Ganguly had been dismissed for a duck, it ran a banner headline on the front page, across the top of the page, making even that feat look somewhat heroic.

You wouldn't think it talking to the man on the street and reading the Bengali papers, but there is among many members of the educated elite in Kolkata a tendency to go against the grain and profess no extra love for Ganguly. (Actually, the way it works is to specifically say that the masses are illogically, irrationally supporting Ganguly. In a way, this stands to reason: Kolkata is a city of self-conscious irony; it is bashfully apologetic about itself and is suffused with a severe abhorrence of self-congratulation in certain circles.)

Several of my friends resort to this sort of thing. I never have. I have always been an admirer of Ganguly's. And I insist that my admiration has nothing to do with being parochial. Nor do I think

I need to go against the grain in this respect to exhibit my distinctiveness from the masses.

But I have been thinking about it. And, you know, I've been asking myself if it is at all possible to entirely divorce parochialism (of some form or the other) from support. Isn't all support a sort of tribalism? Isn't that what it's all *about*? (I mean, I am a big fan of Roger Federer's and John McEnroe's and Diego Maradona's, but with cricket, a sport in which we are actually good? You tell me.)

Well, Bengal's fanaticism about Ganguly *is* to do with parochialism. I am not sure if this is something to be bashfully apologetic about. Sport, you see, as Nick Hornby writes in *The Complete Polysyllabic Spree*, is part of popular culture, however much some of us try to deny it sometimes. And Bengal has been traditionally big on culture—and tremendously proud of it. (If you don't have much else to show— like, say, top industrialists or a lot of money, what else can you do? Culture is your badge of privilege, your only proof of *genuine* distinction.)

Now Bengalis have always had people who would talk about cricket; who would pride themselves on forming the most literate, intelligent cricket crowd in India (a patent lie; I think it went by a name in the popular press—cognoscenti); who would say that the Eden Gardens had the most atmosphere (a nebulous assertion because one isn't

74

quite certain what *atmosphere* might, really, objectively, mean) of all grounds in the world; and who would talk about Kolkata's culture of following cricket in a, well, cultured sort of way.

We had everything, you see. The trouble was, there was no one to follow. We didn't have the players. I mean, okay, Pankaj Roy was from Bengal but to find people who could recall him in his pomp, well, let's just say you won't find too many of them hanging around today at street corners or clubs or bars.

Ganguly fired Bengal's imagination because he was the talisman Bengal had been looking for for decades; he gave people from Kolkata someone to specifically root for. Every state had its players in the national team. Where were Bengal's?

Here was a state that had historically produced nearly no Test players of any stature. In Ganguly, came the answer to years of prayer for a hometown boy who had made good. And how good he made.

But that's not quite why I admire Ganguly. Or at least that is what I *think*.

I think I am a huge Ganguly fan because of the way he has changed Indian cricket. Of how he has changed how players and fans look at it, and how the rest of the world looks at us. It's a staggering achievement, and one that is unparalleled in the history of our game.

Becoming India's Test captain in November 2000, he forged on the anvil of his spectacular, stare-you-in-the-eye-and-not-blink, tough, provocative leadership a side that went from being crumbling-pitch bullies in India to the team that has beaten the (then) world champions, Australia, on more occasions than any other side in this century; the side that has won around the world—in England, the West Indies, Pakistan, South Africa and, of course, Zimbabwe and Bangladesh; the side that has played with audacity and impunity and courage and guts and beauty.

Think about this: Ganguly is India's most successful captain ever but it bears thinking about that the next most successful captain—Mohammed Azharuddin—led India to victory in only one Test away from home, against Sri Lanka in Colombo.

Indian captains were supposed to have been polite, stoic, decent, not overly, demonstrably ambitious, *middle class* in sensibility if not lineage. Ganguly changed all that.

Indian captains before Ganguly were, by and large, known as gracious losers. Which was a decorous way of saying that they didn't want to win enough and didn't protest too much when they lost. Well, they had had enough practice.

But Ganguly was not a gentleman on the field. Nor did he think it was his job to whinge a bit, smile a lot and put up a good show about losing after he had put a show bad enough to have lost in the first place. A scrapper, a hustler, he brought to Indian cricket the sort of chest-thumping, fist-pumping aggression it had never had. Keep Steve Waugh waiting for the toss to needle him? Sure thing. Twirl your shirt on the Lord's balcony as a riposte to Andrew Flintoff? Go ahead.

Ganguly became India captain at around the time that India was established as the new financial powerhouse of the modern game. So he was leading a nation that was at ease with its own exalted status in the sport's pecking order. It is possible that some of his so-called arrogance was a spin-off of his country's newfound status and confidence.

But mostly it was to do with the man himself. He took risks, made brave choices, led from the front as much as pushed from behind and stood by his men when things didn't work out. He was helped by the fact that several great players in the side blossomed into their pomp during his tenure. But he found many new, surprising ones, and welded them together with a team spirit that was rare in Indian cricket. And if he wasn't always tactful with them on the field, they knew that he would not sell them down the river at a selection committee meeting.

He was the fulcrum around which the

contemporary game's premier confrontation in the first decade of the twenty-first century—India v Australia—was built. Indian cricket had always been about supple wrists and flicks off the pad. It had always had a lot of silk. It took Ganguly to put the steel in it.

This has been a thrilling decade—why, a thrilling century, I realize as I write this—to be an Indian cricket fan. And we shall be remiss if we don't acknowledge the extent of Ganguly's contribution to that fact.

It is probably true that his record as captain has somewhat obscured and taken the attention away from his achievements as a batsman. His Test average has never fallen below 40. He is India's fourth-highest Test run scorer and fourth-highest century maker. He has played more Tests than a handful of players in the history of the game, and he has, in them, offered us numerous beautiful, gutsy, unforgettable performances.

Ganguly himself is acutely aware of this fact. On the eve of his last international game, he was quoted as saying (in—where else but?—a Bengali daily) that he has made more than 2000 runs in the past twenty-two Tests. He is very conscious of his stats. And why not? If others aren't, perhaps not as much as they ought to be, the man who made the most stirring comeback in contemporary Indian cricket, ought to be. It's not something to be exactly ashamed of, is it? (Or bashfully apologetic about, perhaps?)

But the fact remains that more than Ganguly the batsman, it is Ganguly the captain (the 'game changer', as the marketing blokes like to call it) I shall remember. And I miss him now that he is no more on the field to remind me of how he did what he did.

~

Rahul Dravid (International Debut: April 1996)

Now isn't the best time to be writing about Rahul Dravid.

The best Number Three batsman that India has ever produced hasn't been having it too good of late. In the winter of 2008 on the eve of the Test series against England at home, one found that the man who was likely to get a big double hundred when most needed scored less than 200 runs in his previous ten Test innings. It was distressing for his admirers to see him—one of the most accomplished batsmen in the history of the international game—in the midst of such a fallow period.

But in a way, this *is* the best time to be writing about Dravid: it's an opportunity to reassess him, and not let the current drought (though he made runs against England and New Zealand) make us lose sight of either the flood of runs he has scored or the true measure of his greatness; also, now that *everyone* is talking about his current lack of success, it's useful to join in and look at the graph that Dravid's appeal has plotted in his own country.

The attention paid to Dravid—even in his pomp, perhaps especially in his pomp—has always been underwhelming. In that, Dravid has been like his fellow legend from Karnataka, Anil Kumble.

Even in the midst of his worst patch, his overall Test average stands at 52. His average in Tests away from home—under unfamiliar, difficult conditions, always the indicator of greatness in a batsman—is *still* at 56, higher than his career average. Which is to say that he has been more successful in arduous conditions than in easy ones. You can't say that for too many players, can you?

And all some of us we can talk about is how long he should be around, and ask if he should be around at all.

Things have always been a bit like that for Dravid ever since that glorious debut in England in 1996. In his first two Tests at Lord's and Trent Bridge, Dravid scored 95 and 84; Sourav Ganguly, who played his first Test alongside him, went on to score centuries in both matches. Dravid was talked about, sure, but Ganguly had run away with all the attention—and most of the plaudits.

Subsequently, Dravid was mucked around with in the one-day side, keeping wickets so that India could play an extra batsman or bowler. He was initially overlooked for the vice-captaincy, before common sense prevailed. And in Kolkata in 2001, we were endlessly talking about Laxman's epic 281, often not giving Dravid's 180 its due, without which one of the most unforgettable fightbacks in the history of the game would not have been possible. See? He scores 180 to win a Test but he still manages to be seen as second fiddle.

It's such a shame, isn't it?

Dravid's achievements have been staggering. Sixteen of his twenty-six Test centuries have been scored overseas; he has Test hundreds in every country in which international cricket is played, and with an unbeaten century against the West Indies at Port of Spain, hundreds in each innings at Headingley and a double century at The Oval in 2003, a double century against Australia in Adelaide in 2003, hundreds against Pakistan in Pakistan in 2004, he has helped win and save more matches for India abroad than any other current batsman.

We know that Sourav Ganguly is India's most successful captain, but do we remember that in the Tests in which he led India to victory, Dravid's average is 100, or thereabouts?

On away tours, when conditions are different in temperament, technique and mettle are called for, Dravid has consistently stood up and delivered more than—whisper this in India—even Tendulkar. As captain he led India to victory against England in England in 2007, winning, after twenty-one years, a series there.

But India—in thrall to Tendulkar with his genius, Ganguly with his leadership qualities and swashbuckle, Virender Sehwag with his bravado and V.V.S. Laxman with his languid elegance—has often looked the other way as Dravid, classical, straight, simple, effective and reliable, has gone on to so often put his peers in the shade.

When Dravid hooked Andy Bichel out of the ground to get to his century during the Adelaide Test in December 2003, it was uncharacteristic. When he did not chase his double century in the same Test so that he could shield Kumble from Gillespie at the end of the day, it was typical.

The first sort of thing is usually seen as fearless adventurism; the second is hardly noticed and, if so, not as warmly applauded as it ought to be. The key to Dravid—and the fact that he is overshadowed by his contemporaries—is that he would, time and again, do the second; he would rarely, if at all, repeat the first.

While reviewing Dravid's biography some years

ago, I was talking to a leading Indian cricket writer. 'I think Dravid is one of the most fascinating figures in modern Indian cricket,' I said. 'Oh no, he is just a regular guy,' my friend replied. 'I mean, where's the back story?"

Well, there you go. Dravid has no chequered past. He is not boorish or arrogant, he is not overtly demonstrative of his feelings, no taint has remotely touched him in fifteen years of international cricket. He is articulate, intelligent and thinks and writes with clarity. 'Regular' is just another way of saying 'boring'.

But boring is the last thing Dravid is. It's worth going miles to see him cover drive off the front foot; his half-hook-half-pull, is as much of a treat as anything in contemporary cricket. He is not dour. He is simply dependable and delightful in an unobtrusive way.

In India, we have too often overlooked the quiet delights of Rahul Dravid. Just imagine: what if he had played for Australia? How miserable would he have made us then?

V.V.S. Laxman (International Debut: November 1996)

In a manner more than perhaps any other player in this current Indian side, V.V.S. Laxman, Janus-faced, looks as much back to a certain kind of Indian cricketer as exemplifies the globalized, post-modern twenty-first-century India. He is firmly rooted in his tradition, in the long lineage of distinguished middle-order Indian batsmen who have killed softly when on song. At the same time, there is about him a sharpness and a modernity, a self-confidence and grim resolve, a solidity in his walk that is informed by the kind of steeliness that Indian cricket has made its own in this century.

I am a huge VVS fan, not least because he conjures up for me memories of the man who was my first sporting hero, Gundappa Viswanath. Like Viswanath's, Laxman's wrists seem to be made of something more elastic than bone and tissue. Like him, neither Laxman's decent, but by no means outstanding, average nor his substantial, but by no means staggering, total of runs is an indicator of his real talent. Underachievers, both of them. But that's not strictly true either. They have both been match-winners, architects of triumph in impossible situations.

An Australian friend of mine recently asked me (this was after VVS gently skewered the Aussies—*again*): 'Why does Laxman bother to get out of bed only for Australia?' It's not entirely accurate, but VVS has been disproportionately successful against the world's best team, an indication as much of his mettle and hunger for the big occasion as for the nature of his achievement.

Numbers aren't everything in this game. How they come about is always central to the story.

And that's the thing with VVS. Unlike some of his predecessors of whom he reminds us, he is not all puckishness and gentle insubstantiality. He gave up a certain career in medicine for an uncertain one in cricket. With his place at stake, he said he would not be a makeshift opener; rather, he would bear being dropped from the side, work on his game and earn his place in the middle order on his own terms.

Laxman is a magical marauder but he can be as sublime with his strokes as he can be infuriating with a suicidal swish outside off stump. It's the swish that has often been the problem.

His first hundred—167 in Sydney in 2000—came in only his 17th Test. His next five Test scores were 16, 0, 18 not out, 20 and 12. The 281 in Kolkata in 2001 (again against Australia, again in an epic Test, again in a game that he largely turned on its head: you see what my Aussie friend was asking, don't you?) was a turning point but he kept on being scintillating and anti-climactic in turns, throwing away starts after gorgeous forties and fifties. He made a century against the West Indies in the Caribbean but continued to be seen as someone who did not value his wicket enough.

The series against Australia in Australia in 2003–04 was Laxman's moment of reckoning: the tour on which he had to prove that he was more than merely a delightful player to watch.

He scored hundreds in Adelaide and Sydney— that is, in two of the four Tests. His 178 in Sydney was especially spectacular, with Sachin Tendulkar, who was at the other end for the entire duration of VVS's innings, saying that Laxman played shots that he never would have dared to.

Watching him hit four boundaries off Brett in an opening session of play, you weren't left merely gasping; you tended to agree with Tendulkar. Characteristically, though, VVS rated neither of the centuries but the 75 in the first innings of the first Test in Brisbane, as his best innings of the series. (If you can, get the DVD.)

So we, his fans, thought it was all sorted, the business about his not valuing his wicket enough. Right, so what did he do next? Here's what: scores of 29, 11 and 13, and no century for the next *five series*.

What can you do when you adore the play of a man who can be as exasperating as that? Well, take what he offers, and count oneself blessed.

Because whenever he bats, Laxman exudes a sense of joy at being at the crease, perhaps a somewhat old-fashioned delight at having fun and seasons in the sun. He rarely seems to construct an innings, block by block. It simply seems to *be there*. He has the unique gift of making the immensely difficult look ludicrously simple; you wonder why more people out there aren't doing it. Laxman is a considerate man: he tries to not trouble fieldsmen. When he splits point and cover with barely a dozen metres between them, neither fielder usually need move.

Laxman can kill as effectively as any contemporary batsman, but he leaves not a drop of blood on the carpet. He plays out his stuff not in the amphitheatre that is the modern game but in an artist's studio. You can almost hear him hum as he works.

It's that song that we thrill to and his opponents quake at the sound of. If only the man could consistently hang on to the tune.

Here
Comes
the
Carnival
Again

April 2009 saw the curtains going up on the second season of the Indian Premier League—a tournament that, in its first edition, had turned out to be one of the most successful experiments in the modern game.

In its first season in the spring and summer of 2008, the IPL saw packed stadiums in nearly every city, an indication that, however much outdated purists like me might sneer at it, a lot of people have taken to this slash-and-burn, smash-and-grab version of the game with tremendous enthusiasm. The second season of the IPL—held in South Africa after security at venues became tricky because the general elections in India were around the same time—was just as much of a success.

Just compare the crowd figures for the India v Australia Test at Nagpur in 2008, the match in which Sachin Tendulkar got his fortieth Test hundred and Sourav Ganguly bid farewell to international cricket with any 2008 IPL game. Sure some tickets were said to have been given away free in the inaugural season, but even then, I suspect, you'll find that there is no comparison. Given the spectator interest and the money raised from advertising and money spent on acquiring the services of certain players, the tournament has shown us glimpses of what the future might hold for cricket.

Till the IPL (and the World Twenty20 Championship in South Africa, and then, in England in 2009), T20 seemed a bit like a puerile distraction. It is now beginning to appear like rather a different proposition.

Some of the stadiums have got better, thanks to this carnival. Facilities for spectators have improved a bit—a much welcome and long-needed development, given that going to the cricket in India must easily be one of the most uncomfortable experiences in spectator sport.

And it has mixed everything up, unveiling a sort of new hierarchy among the players. When clubs' franchisees decided at the outset of the first season Andrew Symonds deserves a hell of a lot more money than, say, Ricky Ponting, for his services, you know that some serious rejigging of priorities is taking place. (Ponting made a lot of jokes about it, but he was shocked at the disparity in what was seen to be his and Symonds's worth to their respective sides.)

For a fan, the one major bewildering conundrum has been the question of loyalty, devoid of which the matter of fandom becomes much diluted. The IPL has begun to ask several serious questions, and it will be a while before we are even close to finding the answers.

As the inaugural IPL season got underway, I reluctantly began to watch some of the games at home. We watched them together, my daughter, then six, and I, as we tend to watch the cricket ('It's social engineering,' one of my friends—her self-appointed godfather—calls this), and I started to notice that there was something bothering her.

It came out on the night of a Kolkata v Mumbai game. Nearly welded to me on the sofa in her customary cricket-watching posture, she frowned, then dilated her eyes and said with grave self-importance: 'But Baba, who should we *support*?'

My daughter and I don't always support the same teams or players. We both go for Arsenal and Argentina in football; but I support Roger Federer and Justine Henin (or used to, before Henin retired) while she roots for Rafael Nadal and Maria Sharapova. But the thing is, there is always someone or some team to throw the weight of our passion behind.

In cricket? Well, that was hardly a question, was it? Till now.

So what happens when it comes to the IPL? Who indeed do we *support*? Because without a genuine allegiance, without there being a true repository of our frenzy, watching sport loses a lot of its (often masochistic) allure.

The question of allegiance between a team and its supporters is unwavering. We're in it for the long haul, and we know it. We'll be there for better or for worse (often for worse), but we'll be *there*.

Till now, deciding which team to support when it came to cricket was more than straightforward for any fan. The IPL has mixed it all up. When the season started (or even before it did), I'd thought I'd support individual players, not a team. Oh, what wouldn't I give to be charmed by Shane Warne waddling in or Muralitharan putting his guile on display? So on a given day, I'd said to myself, I'd root for the team that had my favourite player(s).

Big mistake.

Which team to will on then when Warne bowls to Rahul Dravid?

I went back to thinking about it.

And I realized that for me at least, it would have to be support for the team that bears the name of the place I come from: Kolkata. You can't choose your hometown, just as you can't choose your parents, and wherever you live afterwards and whoever you become, that place remains with you, becomes a part of you in a way like no other.

In a way, it's not so surprising; provenance always decided which team you rooted for in English football. If you came from a particular area of London, you'd support West Ham; if you came from another, you'd go for Arsenal.

This was of course before the English Premier League, midwifed by astonishing amounts of money (like the IPL), was born, before the attitude of wanting to be closely identified with success—and super-successful, glamorous sides—became reason enough to support a team.

Nowadays, a boy who hasn't grown up anywhere near Chelsea could support Chelsea. The team, with some of the best players in the world, has its own cachet. (Perhaps that is how it will go with the IPL as well, but now, the matter of support is turning out to be more atavistic than anything else.)

Glamour or success, though, wasn't how allegiance used to be determined in English football once upon a time. One would previously stand by one's home team, however crap it was, and endure games in rain and sleet and snow to watch them be humiliated—*again*.

Julian Barnes, one of England's finest living novelists, once described how and why he supports Leicester City, a thoroughly and determinedly unsuccessful football side: 'Leicester City are my team because I was born there, though we moved to London six weeks later,' he told the *Observer Sport Monthly* in 2001. (I mean, *six weeks*? Oh, my god. I'm doing better here.) 'Starting to support them when I was four or five was a sentimental way of hanging on to Leicester. An emotional bond is formed at an early age and, unless you are a complete tart and transfer to a rich side, you stick with your childhood team.'

It isn't merely English football. Indian cricket fans old enough to remember a time when our first-class game mattered anything at all, a time when Test players actually captained zonal teams and the Ranji and Duleep Trophies were followed with fervour, will recognize the same impulse at play while determining support. (If there's anyone from Mumbai who supported South Zone or anyone from Bangalore who rooted for West Zone, I'd like to know.)

In the case of the IPL, a lot of fans—like me— would not have had the chance for these bonds to be formed at a young age. At the same time, a lot of fans—like my daughter—would. And provenance is perhaps the way it is most likely to go—for now.

I'm not sure that that's how it will be for, say, Mohali or Bangalore, but that's how it will be for Kolkata. (Apart from everything else, it was a marketing masterstroke to get Sourav Ganguly— who really doesn't deserve to be in *any* Twenty20 side—to lead the Kolkata team.) Kolkata (as we have seen earlier on in this book) has a unique relationship with Ganguly. His presence truly engenders and strengthens the fan's bond with the side.

But mostly, I suppose, it's to do with the nature of the place—and its sons and daughters. The Kolkatan, with his passive-aggressiveness, his implicit assumptions of his own cultural superiority, his bashful-yet-confident love for his own city, his apologetic, ironical view of himself and his hometown's place in the scheme of things, is city-proud in a way no other Indian is.

I live in Mumbai these days, after having lived in half-a-dozen cities in India and abroad. I've found that the Mumbaikar is tremendously city-proud too. But for the large part, he is too blinkered, too insular, too chest-thumpingly self-congratulatory about Mumbai to allow for the refined ambiguities of irony and self-deprecation.

So, to the extent that I cared anything at all for the IPL, Kolkata it was for me during the two seasons. I suspect it will be again in the spring and summer of 2010. Will it be like that for my daughter? Will she, as she grows older, identify herself more closely with Mumbai? Will she simply switch to the most glamorous, successful side? It's too early to tell. It will depend, I suppose, as much on her as on how the IPL carnival unfolds in the years to come.

I told my daughter as much that evening. 'I'm going for Kolkata. That's where I am from, you see. How about you?'

Too confused by these new loyalties to argue, she pumped her little fist, and said: 'Yaay.'

At least something had been resolved. We were on it, supporting the same team, both of us.

That evening, we watched Kolkata getting stuffed by Mumbai—a team that had as yet won not a single game. It felt like familiar territory. As an India fan, I've had enough practice.

But I noticed something afterwards. When discussing the game with people, I kept saying 'Kolkata got clobbered', rather than 'We got clobbered'. 'We' is what I'd always say when talking about the Indian cricket team.

When it comes to the IPL—and me watching it—the line between the fan and his team hasn't yet got blurred. And I am not sure it ever will. It's *very* early days yet.

Field
of
Dreams

TV first introduced me to cricket in the summer of 1974. I was four years old, and living with my parents in a flat on Bolsover Street in west London. The TV itself was an object of wonder for me. I had never seen one before (remember, this was still 1974 and India, when I left it for England with my parents a year previously, was a long way off from having television).

I was of course no stranger to the radio but the fact that you could merely flick a switch and bring into your home moving pictures and sound at the same time seemed magical. I would gaze enraptured at the set in our living room even when it was turned off; I would stare unblinking at it just after it had been switched off, watching the screen lose its glow, become a dimming speck of gradually vanishing light.

And when it was on? Well, I was in front of it for as long as I could.

One of the big things on TV that summer was India's tour of England. Or at least it was for my parents. India arrived in England, after having beaten in the past three years, the West Indies in the West Indies and England at home and away. London in the 1970s was not quite the multiracial, multicultural world capital that it is today; and no one could have imagined then that India would three decades later be seen as an emerging world power. My parents had little to show off to their English friends and colleagues as contemporary Indian achievement and glory. They—a couple in their thirties from one of the world's poorest countries, my father trying to make his way in a white-collar profession like medicine in London—were hoping that the Indian cricket team would exemplify the best that India had to offer.

The series showed how misguided their hopes were.

India lost the first Test at Old Trafford by 113 runs. In the second at Lord's—which unfolded not very far from where we lived—India were so abject that it was thumped by an innings and 285 runs. Following on, they were all out for 42 in the second innings. The summer of '74 began to be called the 'Summer of 42'.

It was the first series that I had ever followed, and it was good training. It was appropriate preparation for the years of torment that were to follow: of waking up at 3 a.m. and watch us getting a pasting; of staying up the whole night and watch us getting thrashed; of skiving off work (or school or family responsibilities) to see us savaged, decimated, humiliated, murdered.

I didn't know then, but a lifetime of misery lay ahead of me.

I found out bit by bit as I began to realize that I was in this for good. It happened through listening to cricket commentary on a reliable, well-travelled Grundig radio in Bankura, a small, backwater town in Bengal in which I lived with my parents for a little less than two years. (The radio was a wedding present; my parents took it with them wherever they went.) There was Test Match Special on short-wave, commentary in rich, plummy accents and often incomprehensible jokes that made me create for myself a vision of what it must seem like to watch cricket at Lord's with the slope of the Nursery End in front of me. (I later realized how wrong I'd been on first visiting Lord's as a spectator. Distance had bred enchantment as only distance can, and the radio—and my age, six—had allowed me to mythologize the experience as only six-year-olds can.) There was commentary—at all odd hours of the day and night—when India toured Australia or the West Indies. And there was commentary from games played in India. The reception would vary, the sound sometimes crackle and fade, but I kept my ears to the radio, sometimes giving it a good shake or slap when the sound waned. Often, it worked.

Kolkata, the closest venue for the international cricket that I heard relayed, was a couple of hundred kilometres away. But my love for cricket blossomed in Bankura precisely because I was so far away from any real action.

I became obsessed with the game through radio commentary and pictures in black-and-white magazines and epic re-enactments of whole Tests in our backyard. (Single-handed. Not only playing on behalf of both teams by throwing a ball against the wall and hitting it, but also keeping a running commentary and cheering resoundingly if things were going well for India. Which they usually did because the flow of the match and its outcome were in my hands.)

You didn't go out with friends in Bankura. (There was nowhere to go to.) You didn't watch TV. (There was no television.) You didn't listen to music. (There was no music store to buy tapes from.) You didn't go to the cinema. (There was one cinema in the town and not once, in the two years that I spent there, did they show anything remotely resembling a film which my parents thought was suitable for me.) You didn't read much. (The two bookstores sold school textbooks. Anything else had to be brought back from Kolkata on our occasional visits.)

As entertainment, the cricket was all that there was for me. And what could one do but make it my life?

Soon enough, I got close to real action. I first went to the Eden Gardens when the West Indies came to play in the winter of 1978. And then went for every international game there, for a quarter of a century. As the years rolled by, the options of how to follow cricket multiplied. It became a veritable buffet, an unfolding of a panoply of delights: TV began live telecasts; satellite TV arrived; the Internet came along with its ball-by-ball and podcasts from experts; and the glut of sports channels began their telecasts of nearly every match that was being played in any corner of the globe, and the endless re-runs of famous matches and splendid innings.

Sometimes it seems hard to escape cricket in India. Fans like me—especially the older ones, the fans who are middle class, not far away from middle age, socially active and parents, the ones who need to strip away all the clutter, arrange their schedules so that they can make space in their lives for the cricket—aren't complaining.

We can't get enough of it. The cricket reminds us of things in our pasts; it is one of the greatest pleasures of the lives we lead now; and it will be crucial—and here I can speak only for myself—to the future. (More of that in a minute.)

In the summer of 2006, I published my first book, a memoir about being an Indian cricket fan. I put myself on the line to do this, to explore the troubling hold that cricket has over me, and more than a billion other of my countrymen. I worried at the time about something Nick Hornby—who was a big influence—had written about towards the end of *Fever Pitch*, his memoir about being an Arsenal fan.

'There was a part of me that was afraid to write all this down in a book,' Hornby writes, 'just as a part of me was afraid to explain to a therapist precisely what it had all come to mean: I was worried that by doing so it would all go, and I'd be left with this great big hole where football used to be.'

I was deeply concerned about whether the writing of my book would take the edge off this great love, and worried about that continually during the writing. That hasn't happened, and, by now, I am reasonably sure that it won't. (That is one of the reasons why I agreed to write this sort-of sequel.)

Something else has happened, though. Having a growing child to whom I am devoted and attentive, living in a city in which we have no support structure in terms of the extended family and having a day job that is terribly demanding and consuming, the time I have for cricket has been cut down. I yearn for it as much; I long for the time when I could spare all my time for the five days of a Test; but I really need to make time to watch, uninterrupted, the game that has for so long and in so many ways defined my life—and the lives of so many Indians.

It's like this. As an impoverished student in London in the early 1990s, I made, on a whim, a trip back to Kolkata to simply yield to the desire that had suddenly usurped my life: to watch a game at the Eden Gardens.

In December 2007, at the end of the first day's play of the India–Pakistan Test at the Eden, I found that India had racked up 352 for the loss of three wickets. Wasim Jaffer was not out on 192, and Sourav Ganguly on 17. V.V.S. Laxman, a man with a soft spot for the Eden, and the man for whom the spectators there had a very soft spot, was to follow the next day. Driving back home from work, I suddenly began to feel the keen, slightly unsettling urge of wanting to be at the stadium the following morning.

What if they both score hundreds? What a moment that would be! Shouldn't I *be* there? *Why* shouldn't I? By the time I was turning into the lane on which we live, I had more or less made up my mind. Take a late-night flight. Or an early-morning one. The following day was a Saturday. Take the day off from work. Be back on Sunday. God knew I could afford it now, unlike when I travelled thousands of miles from London.

A couple of hours later, I had abandoned the idea. There was a parent–teacher meeting at our daughter's school. We had invited people over for dinner (I'd forgotten). Somebody was bunking at work, and I really needed to go in. And so on. Just as important; what if Ganguly went in the first over of play, and VVS failed to get into double figures. No point. I didn't go.

In the event, Ganguly scored 102; VVS made 112 not out. And watching it on TV, nursing a beer and having my breath being taken away by their stroke play, I felt like a wimp. It was a bit like letting your love down.

If something like this had happened fifteen years ago, I would have mooched around for days, for *weeks* and would have taken years to contemplate forgiving either myself or the other people responsible for depriving me of this experience.

This time around, I felt deprived; but then, I shrugged to myself, and got on with things. (However, under a cloud of resentment against I

wasn't sure exactly what, my Sunday was ruined.)
How things change.

Some things have not changed at all. Even now, when
I watch the game broadcast from Australia, I think
of the first time I watched on TV cricket played in
Australia, a country—like several other ones—I then
defined solely in terms of its cricket grounds. It was
over February and March 1985. It was the Benson
and Hedges World Championship of Cricket.

Remember the bikinis? When I think now of
what I remember most about first watching cricket
played in Australia, it seems to be the bikinis. But
that tournament itself was thrilling. India won,
beating Pakistan in a day–night final. Ravi Shastri
emerged as champion of champions and took the
team on a ride around the MCG on the Audi that
was his prize. For me, a teenager watching in the
living room of our south Kolkata home, in a
not-so-liberal, not-at-all liberalized India, seeing a
car like the Audi—and the fact that an Indian sporting
hero could now possess it—was a thrill. But the
sight of all those toned female bodies and the
Channel 9 cameras lingering over them in their
jokey, nudge-nudge-wink-wink slow tracks was a
far bigger, almost illicit thrill.

Of course, there was the magnificent Channel 9 coverage. A whole generation of Indian cricket fans growing up in the 1970s had never ever seen anything like that before. Used—and that only just—to Doordarshan's stodgy, boring, shot-from-one-angle stuff and execrable commentary, the manner in which cricket could be brought alive on TV, made spectator-friendly, participatory and exciting was a revelation. Angles, cameras, experts, debates, urgency, the *details*: how I loved it. It seemed like justification for being a fan.

I watched India's 2007–08 tour to Australia on TV at my Mumbai home. (The one before that, I had seen at grounds in Australia—an absolute carnival of celebration, of leisurely delight.) I no longer find the bikinis as much of a novelty as I used to. Also, frankly, not half as much of an attraction. And with the technical sophistication in the coverage of cricket in India now about world-class, Channel 9 doesn't seem *that* different any longer. (In any case, I don't watch Channel 9 at home.)

A lot has changed. But there is one thing that is common even now to my first experiences of watching cricket in Australia: the unrivalled pleasure of getting up in the morning to watch the game. Could anything be better, quite so unsullied an enjoyment? I go to sleep in delicious anticipation, looking forward to waking up and watching. I start the day with the game, mind uncluttered, nothing having yet happened to ruin my day or mood.

I go to bed with the remote on my bedside table. Wake up and smell the coffee? No, wake up and watch the cricket. It's much more invigorating.

I know there are millions who do the same thing, who feel the same way. Perhaps you—having come so far with this book—do too.

As I get older it becomes ever more apparent that cricket is a window on to a different universe. Its disappointments do not have a bearing on my job or my family; its thrills are otherworldly. I need only to press a button on my remote, and I will be transported.

On bad days, I have a fantasy in which I'm much older. I often find myself imagining the worst. My career's over (as the years goes by that's something that becomes less and less difficult to envisage); I have arthritis or some other debilitating but not life-threatening illness which leaves me just about housebound; my daughter has left home, my parents are dead, my wife no longer finds me an amusing or interesting companion; and I no longer write or get published, so reading becomes less of a motivation and delight.

What will I be left with then? Should such an eventuality come to pass (and with life, you just never can tell), I know I will always have the cricket. At the flick of a switch and the turning of a knob, with the riffle of a newspaper or the click of a mouse, I will be able to summon those familiar images, those thrills, that other world.

When I was young, I never thought of these things—one doesn't think of growing old when one is a child. Now I fear the loneliness that age might bring. And I hug cricket to myself because one day it may be all that's left me.

I wrote much of this book in the early-morning quiet of my Mumbai home. I welcomed those hours of introspective silence (the trade-off was that I had to often compromise on my daily walks. But then, you can't have everything.) My daughter would be off at school. My wife would potter about in those rare hours that she has to herself. These are hours I have to myself too before the ebb and flow of the day begins to tug at me.

The morning after India won the one-day international tri-series against Australia in Australia in 2008, beating Australia for the second time in four days. I wanted—as almost always—to relive the thrill of a huge win. It's not merely me; I know there are so many others all over India who do it too.

So I closed my eyes and saw them again, our boys from the white-hot Australian summer, sprinting across the Gabba in Brisbane as though they would never want time to catch up with them. Sreesanth with the tricolour and his exaggerated, faux-movie star air; Harbhajan, twirling his souvenir stump above his head, thumping his chest; Dhoni, as composed in his bearing as his batting is unfettered, trying not to show how overwhelming the moment is; and Praveen Kumar, the young find, the surprise package, the man of the match, with a goofy grin that suggests he can't believe that he is the star of the sort of spectacle he used to watch on TV.

The day's papers were in front of me. The *Hindustan Times* had put out a photo feature on how fans in Mumbai watched the game, and how they celebrated. There was a group of young boys in Shivaji Park (where Sunil Gavaskar and Tendulkar played when they were children), in cricket gear, bats held triumphantly aloft, faces creased in smiles of the unalloyed delight that only children can experience. There was a photograph of a set of smartly dressed young men, their drinks on the table, letting out a collective whoop of joy at a club in Mumbai's western suburbs. And there was a photograph of a crowd packed tight on the pavement, gnawed by suspense, watching the game outside a jewellery store. The crush was so great that some of them, even after craning their necks, could probably see merely the score at the bottom of the TV screen inside. Some looked like students, some like travelling salesmen, some like odd-jobs men.

My eye was riveted by a man right at the periphery of the crowd. His arms were bent, one raised, the other stretched out. Between them he supported on his shoulder what looked like a very heavy cardboard box. He must have been on his way to deliver it somewhere. He stood rooted to the spot, uncomfortably rooted, but his eyes fixed on the TV—or the little of it that he could see from where he was standing. He could not tear himself away. Work could wait, so could making a living. For the moment, in the tense moments of a critical match, the cricket was all that mattered, it was all he had, or wanted to care about.

The rest of life? That could happen between overs.

It's a typically Indian story: Cricket as participatory spectacle, as street theatre, as catharsis, as a field of dreams.

Afterword

Afterword

I haven't watched all that much cricket in 2009. India hasn't played that much. Or, to be more accurate, India hasn't played that much Test cricket—which is the sort of thing I most enjoy.

Certainly, there was the away series in New Zealand in the first part of the year. And what a series that was. A win against the Kiwis in New Zealand after 33 years, even allowing for the diminished nature of the hosts' side, was something to feel genuinely triumphant about. But that was it, really.

Some of us had kept asking—looking at our consistent resurgence and Australia's suddenly fallible nature—if India could (would?) emerge as the best team in the world in 2009. But then, you have a chance to go for that crown only if you are playing the top teams. We played only New Zealand, and so that question remained—tantalizingly, alas—merely posed, not answered.

Indian players played a hell of a lot of cricket, though. There were meaningless one-day series halfway across the world. There were international Twenty20 tournaments (we'll come to one of those in a bit). And, of course, among them, was Season 2 of the IPL. Which, a lot of people (especially a lot of people who have no time for the sort of cricket that I adore) seemed to have rather enjoyed.

After the conclusion of the second season of the IPL, the business newspaper, *Mint*, reported how ESPN Star Sports—the broadcaster that later beamed the ICC World Twenty20 Championships in June— had raised its advertising rates by 80 per cent this year. For a ten-second spot, the advertiser now had to pay about US$8000—up from around US$4500. On the eve of the tournament, the channel expected to raise almost US$50 million in advertising from the championship.

This again proves the primacy of cricket in our national culture. It is evidence—if any more were needed—that for as long as there is cricket (*any* form of it will eventually do), it will continue to be India's Number One game.

Cricket will have to change to stay alive and relevant, and it is in any case the most flexible, the continuously changing of games. (How many revolutions have you seen in football? Think of cricket thirty years ago, and look at it now. Often, it seems unrecognizable from what it used to be.) And cricket will change. None of us—administrators, fans, players—will threaten its existence in our lives by being rigid, and not letting it adapt to the times.

But the IPL's success does not mean—as some people have facilely concluded—that Test cricket is in any danger of being removed from its undisputed pedestal as the premier form of the game. Not yet, not for a while to come. If the success of Twenty20 threatens any format of the game, it is perhaps one-day cricket. There is no sign yet of that happening, but the twenty-over-a-side is at least remotely comparable to the fifty-overs version. They are distant cousins; the former is a whittled down, far more crowd-pleasing version of the other.

Twenty20 and Tests? They aren't related. They simply aren't the same game. And Tests continue to draw a massive, loyal supporter base. Outside the subcontinent, especially in England and Australia, stadiums still sell out—or are close to being full—during Tests. When the first Ashes Test was played at Cardiff in July 2009, there was not a seat empty on any of the five days: It was the same for each of the four Tests that followed in the series.

In India and Pakistan and Sri Lanka, though, Tests are not as well attended as they used to be twenty-five years ago. First, the stadiums do nothing to make you want to go. They are among the worst in the world (they still are, in spite of their having got a little better after the start of the IPL), and the fan, let alone getting value for money, gets barely any respect for having paid to watch the game. He is made to feel as unwelcome as possible; and he is forced to think of being at the cricket as an uncomfortable privilege.

No wonder they do not want to come—not for every day for five days, for the whole day (no day-night Tests yet, although if the ICC takes a decision that it is pondering over, that might before long be part of the game's changing fabric), in the baking heat, sitting on concrete steps in often uncovered stands.

Fans had been looking for an alternative: TV gave them that. With the cricket beamed live, they could watch Tests at home, in the office, in comfort, with food and drink and friends. And the coverage got better and better. There were replays. It seemed like a better choice when one didn't—one inescapably did ever so often—have the itch to sit high in the stands and see the players in the flesh and for the action to seem thrillingly *real*.

There is more evidence to show that Test cricket continues to be rather more popular than some of its doomsayers would have themselves believe. The money no longer comes merely from bums on seats. (Which could be why Indian cricket administrators have been so unpardonably callous in terms of providing spectators basic comforts at stadiums.) The money is in the number of people watching on TV, which determines how much the big companies will spend on ads between overs and in the stadiums. That seems to be, as Kadambari Murali pointed out in the *Hindustan Times*, in pretty good health.

The average Television Viewership Rating (TVR) for the India v New Zealand series in 2009 was 1.2–2. And this for a not particularly high-profile series, with play beginning at 3 a.m. IST every day. Many serials have a TVR of between 0.5 and 3.

When India travelled to Australia in 2007–08, ESPN-STAR averaged 3.12 for the series. The riveting fourth Test rated 4.24—higher than the 4.2 that was the average of IPL's second season.

Test cricket, as that piece bore out, could—again, in keeping with its ever-changing nature—well be on its way towards becoming the world's most followed sport on the Internet. Hundreds of thousands of people at work are logging in to catch the ball-by-ball commentary on websites. The Guardian's OBO (over-by-over) has become an institution, fostering arguments, banter and sharing of anecdotes and memories in the way a group of people once would while listening to the commentary on the radio.

Cricinfo, the world's most popular cricket website, recorded its biggest day ever both in India (687,666 unique users) and across the world

(1,798,702 unique users) on 10 November 2008—the final day of the India v Australia Test in Nagpur.

So Test matches are still very much being looked forward to, followed and enjoyed. Ignoring the fact that they aren't being followed in the manner that they used to be thirty years ago, or the fact that the manner in which their revenue model has changed, is to be not merely philistine; it is to be blinkered about the way in which the world has changed.

But it has. What to do? It doesn't mean Tests are going away in the immediate future. They won't as long as the manner in which they currently make money remains viable; as long as people in some countries continue to pack to the grounds; and certainly for as long as Ricky Ponting (or any other Australian captain) would much rather win the Ashes than the World Twenty20 Championship, and Yuvraj Singh (or any other feted Indian tyro) would give his left hand to score fifteen Test hundreds rather than cart sixes in a silly IPL tournament.

England hosted the 2009 World Twenty20 Championship. Which brings me to the part that I found most reassuring in the year's cricketing events. Which also brings us—again—to the patterns that we fans love so much. This book opened with India's unexpected—and unexpectedly giddying—victory in Johannesburg in the inaugural World Twenty20 championship in 2007. How appropriate that it should close with India's shambolic performance in 2009, a tournament we were, for a change, expected to go and win.

No Indian fan in his teens now will remember a proper international tournament (a sort of world cup, really) in which India went in as defending champion and favourite to retain the title. Before the start of the tournament, the British bookmaker, Ladbrokes, had made us the odds-on favourite. All the talk in India as well as in England was of who could stand in India's way. Dhoni and his team (shorn of the Fab Five) had about it an aura of inevitable success.

This was not expectation as someone like me, who has followed Indian cricket for more than three decades now, knew it. For a lot of Indian supporters, it seemed a foregone conclusion that their team would win. Here was a sense of the final exultation being held in abeyance.

Moved by the frenzied hype, I watched every India game till the end. (This—four matches—is the most number of Twenty20 games I have ever watched on the trot. It is about the most I have the stomach for.) Sure, I knew this was only Twenty20, but then, the novelty of the situation was overwhelming.

Defending champions and undisputed favourites? *Us*? Come, come . . .

India failed to go beyond the first round. It won only one of four games it played. That was against Bangladesh. And it was walloped by South Africa, thrashed by West Indies and decimated by England. Some of its stars who had come through the IPL (like Ravinder Jadeja) were shown up to be amateurs when playing against international teams.. Others, like Rohit Sharma, were sussed out against the short rising ball and made to appear embarrassments. Soon after the defeat, the recriminations started.

The response was predictable, and predictably hyperbolic. Watching it on TV and reading about it in the papers, I was reminded of Martin Amis writing about the critical revisionism that followed the death of Philip Larkin, one of England's greatest postwar poets.

'The reaction,' Amis wrote, 'like most reactions, is just an overreaction. To get an overreaction, you need plenty of overreactors. Somebody has to do it. And here they all are, overreacting.'

Well, here we all were, too, overreacting. Why was I not surprised in the least?

Dhoni's men—sombre, humiliated and, used

only to adoration, now at the receiving end of resentful criticism and derision, were made acutely aware of their feet of clay.

For me, all this seemed very familiar, even comforting. It was the deliriousness and the triumphs and triumphalism of the past two years that had seemed disquieting. Me, I was used to not daring to hope, of, on occasions, allowing myself to hope, and of more often than not having those hopes thwarted, of living with gloom and misery at yet another failure.

That seemed to me what following India was all about. *That* was normal service. We had been living in a bubble for nearly two years. It was a question of when it would burst. Now we were back on well-known turf. For me, who has seen India win far fewer games than lose, it seemed like a sort of sad but authentic homecoming.

In 1948, the American writer E.B. White wrote a moving, insightful homage to New York in the pages of the *Holiday* magazine. A year later, the 7500-word essay was published as a slim book. In his foreword to the book, White noted the changes that had come about in New York in the year that the essay first appeared in the magazine.

'The reader will find certain observations to be no longer true of the city, owing to the passage of time and the swing of the pendulum,' he wrote. 'But the essential fever of New York has not changed in any particular, and I have not tried to make revisions in the hope of bringing the thing down to date . . . I feel that it is the reader's, not the author's, duty to bring New York down to date; and I trust it will prove less a duty than a pleasure.'

I have thought again and again of White's piece while winding up this book. Writing about being an Indian cricket fan is a tricky business. No sooner have you written something than that something changes, it becomes something else, is overtaken by events; the story has not so much moved on since the time of writing, but is continually moving on. Too much can change in Indian cricket in too little time.

But I have not—to borrow White's phrase—tried to make revisions in the hope of bringing the thing down to date. (Love the quaint Americanism of bringing it *down* to date.)

This is a book about India, and around cricket, and how that one game defines us as a nation and how my story of being a fan of that game, that team, is emblematic of that of hundreds of thousands of you, and I think that however much the story of

Indian cricket might have moved on, the ardour and the passion—what White calls 'the essential fever'—has not and will not change.

The bringing down to date of the story, I am hoping, fans will continue to do in bars and clubs and stadiums and street corners and offices and schools.

Like White, I trust it will prove less a duty than a pleasure.

Mumbai
August 2009

Acknowledgements

Certain sections of this book appeared, in somewhat different forms, as parts of essays published in the *Hindustan Times*, the *Sydney Morning Herald*, Cricinfo and the *Observer* (London).

I owe the title of this volume to my favourite U2 album.

I should like to thank Udyan Mitra, Aakash Chakrabarty and everyone else at Penguin Books India for the way in which this little book has turned out.

Its inadequacies are all mine.